World Health Organization
Regional Office for Europe
Copenhagen

Alcohol and the workplace

by

Marion Henderson,
Graeme Hutcheson
and John Davies
Centre for Applied Social Psychology,
University of Strathclyde,
Glasgow,
United Kingdom

WHO Regional Publications, European Series, No. 67

WHO Library Cataloguing in Publication Data

Henderson, Marion
    Alcohol and the workplace / by Marion Henderson, Graeme Hutcheson, John Davies

    (WHO regional publications. European series ; No. 67)

    1.Alcohol drinking 2.Alcoholism - prevention and control 3.Occupational health
    4.Workplace 5.Europe I.Davies, John II.Hutcheson, Graeme III.Title IV.Series

    ISBN 92 890 1331 1   (NLM Classification: WM 274)
    ISSN 0378-2255

The Regional Office for Europe of the World Health Organization welcomes requests for permission to reproduce or translate its publications, in part or in full. Applications and enquiries should be addressed to the Office of Publications, WHO Regional Office for Europe, Scherfigsvej 8, DK-2100 Copenhagen Ø, Denmark, which will be glad to provide the latest information on any changes made to the text, plans for new editions, and reprints and translations already available.

©World Health Organization 1996

PRINTED IN FINLAND

Acknowledgements

The authors acknowledge the generous help freely provided by organizations and people too numerous to mention individually. The following, however, deserve special thanks.

Peter Anderson, WHO Regional Office for Europe; Rik Bijl, Stichting Alcohol Consultancy, Zeist, Netherlands; Judith Billingham, Alcohol Concern, Wales; Richard Brooks, Department of Economics, Strathclyde University; Elizabeth Cain, Department of Health, Housing, Local Government and Community Services, Canberra, Australia; City of Liverpool Development and Environmental Services Directorate; Jorge Coutinho, Centro Regional de Alcoologia do Porto, Portugal; Alex Crawford, Director, Renfrew Council on Alcohol; Richard Cyster, Regional Alcohol Coordinator, Regional Service Development Centre, Leeds; Adrian Davies, Maureen McClelland and Ivan Miller, Scottish and Glasgow Councils on Alcohol; Cécile Delmarcelle, Orée Communications, Brussels; John Duffy, University of Edinburgh; Andy Fox, Centre for Applied Social Psychology, Strathclyde University; Jean J. Franck, Conseil National Luxembourgeois d'Alcoologie, Luxembourg; Andrea Hutcheson, Priory Hospital, Scotland; Angela Kerigan, Centre of Applied Social Psychology, Strathclyde University; Scott Macdonald, Addiction Research Foundation, Canada; John Marsden, Turning Point, London; M.T. Pérez Martínez, APTA, Madrid; Andrew McNeil, Institute of Alcohol Studies, London; Jacek Morawski, Alcohol and Drug Information Centre, Warsaw; Jacek Moskalewicz, Institute of Psychiatry and Neurology, Poland; Joyce O'Connor, National College of Industrial Relations Limited, Dublin; Alastair J. Ross, Centre for Applied Social Psychology, Strathclyde University; Martina Rummel, Projekt Alkohol am Arbeitsplatz, Landesstell gegen die Suchtgefahren e.V. Berlin, Germany; Edward Sawka, Alberta Alcohol and Drug Abuse Commission, Canada; Les Schäfer, Hamburg University; Behrouz Shahandeh, International Labour Office, Geneva; William J. Staudenmeier, Eureka College, Illinois, USA; Advisory Council on Alcohol and Drug Education, London; Konstantin von Veitinghoff-Scheel, Corporate Caring Systems, Brussels; Linda B. Wright, Centre for Applied Social Psychology, Strathclyde University; and Uglijesa Zvekic, United Nations Interregional Crime and Justice Research Institute, Italy.

Contents

Introduction

Alcohol is the most widely used drug in the world today and is an integral part of the social, cultural and economic life of many countries. In Australia, for example, it is estimated that 74% of males and 52% of females drink alcohol *(1)*. This incidence is similar to that found in the United States, where it has been estimated that in 1988 some 68% of males and 47% of females were regular drinkers *(2,3)*. The proportion of people who drink alcohol in the European Union, where there is a much more established drinking culture, is considerably higher than these estimates, with studies indicating that 85% of all citizens over 15 years of age drink alcohol. Within this group, as in other countries, a higher proportion of males drink alcohol, with estimates of the proportion who drink being around 90% *(4)*.

Given the physiological and behavioural effects that alcohol consumption can have, such widespread use is of considerable concern. This concern can be seen in *The health of the nation,* the health policy for England *(5),* which outlines a number of health targets to be met in the future. These targets involve a reduction in the incidence of heart disease, stroke, cancers and accidents, and an improvement in sexual and mental health. Alcohol, which is designated as one of the risk factors in the report, is implicated in all of the above-mentioned targets. It is not surprising, therefore, that there is an explicit aim to achieve by the year 2005 a 30% reduction in the number of people who drink more than the recommended safe limits (21 units of alcohol a week for men and 14 for women). There is also considerable international concern about the potentially damaging health effects of alcohol consumption, as the following quotation *(6)* demonstrates.

In 1980 the European Member States adopted a common health policy as a regional strategy to achieve health for all by the year 2000. In 1984 the WHO Regional Committee for Europe followed this up by endorsing 38 targets describing the minimum progress that the European countries must make in improving health and health-related problems ... Alcohol is involved in 12 of the 38 targets in one way or another, notably in target 17 which reads: 'By the year 2000, the health-damaging consumption of dependence-producing substances such as alcohol, tobacco and psychoactive drugs should have been significantly reduced in all Member States'.

Alcohol use is likely to have consequences for industry, as it is clear from a number of estimates that alcohol consumers comprise the majority of the working population. Alcohol use can be particularly serious within the workplace, as it has an impact on human performance that can affect, for example, productivity, accident rates, working relationships and absenteeism. The potential costs associated with alcohol consumption within the workplace have recently been highlighted by research and in health campaigns, as well as through the hypothesized contribution of alcohol consumption to a number of high-profile industrial accidents. The perceived negative role of alcohol consumption within the workplace is therefore of concern to employers, and has led to the introduction of policies that aim to ban or at least to control alcohol consumption.

This review is specifically aimed at investigating the effects of alcohol consumption on the workplace and the types of action that companies take with regard to this issue. An attempt has been made to examine the available literature relating to alcohol consumption in the workplace in as open-ended and dispassionate a manner as possible. As required by any endeavour that would claim to be "scientific", the aim is to be objective, to check our own interpretations against those of others, and to reduce as far as possible the impact of personal views and ideas on the subject. We are aware, none the less, of the difficulties in bringing such an approach to this subject. It is clear that the issues of alcohol consumption at work, and workplace policies on alcohol-related problems, involve at some level a number of ethical and moral judgements or beliefs. To a lesser extent we are also aware that different individuals' political orientation probably has an impact on the type of interventions or policies favoured.

HISTORICAL OVERVIEW

Understanding something of the history of alcohol use is a useful introduction to current issues surrounding the use and control of alcohol within the workplace.

The importance and value attached to alcohol historically can be seen, to some extent, in its use as a form of currency. Before the Industrial Revolution in Russia, for example, vodka was used as a cash substitute when there was a scarcity of money, a practice also believed to have occurred in other regions including England, continental Europe, and the British colonies in the Americas. Even when cash was available, there was some advantage for employers paying their labourers in kind because of the difference between real and nominal values (7). Alcohol was also used to attract alcohol-dependent people to labour-intensive jobs in times when labour was scarce.

Warner (8) claims that, far from being a negative influence, alcohol may have served to increase productivity in that it helped labourers to work long hours in often extremely unpleasant conditions. Such use of alcohol appears similar to the way that drugs such as coca leaves (in Peru) and cannabis (in Jamaica) have been used in relation to hard physical labour. Whether or not alcohol *actually* improved productivity as Warner claims, it was at least *perceived* to do so. The traditional beliefs about alcohol that supported its use by workers included protection against extremes of heat and cold, promotion of vigorous work, and the prevention of disease. Because of such beliefs, many workers from the seventeenth to the nineteenth centuries were reluctant to work without it (7). Encouragement, or at least the implicit acceptance, of the use of alcohol at work therefore has a long history.

The Industrial Revolution of the nineteenth century encouraged employers to invest huge amounts of money in industrial plants and machinery, thus bringing about a need for large, trained workforces that could work regular hours. The imposition of tightly organized working practices was difficult if workers consumed excessive amounts of alcohol on and off the job. Employers were therefore motivated to control their employees' drinking through changing the "work and social habits, attitudes and lifestyles of the labouring class" in an attempt to aid the industrialization process *(9)*. The Industrial Revolution is often identified as one of the factors that gave impetus to the establishment of widespread drinking controls, and can be viewed as a catalyst for the establishment of the temperance movements that sprang up in a number of countries *(10)*.

The Industrial Revolution also provides the historical basis for a number of different perceptions of the respective roles of employers and employees within the general employment setting – roles that have important implications for the establishment of health-related policies. There is ample evidence from historical sources of inhumane and exploitative practices in the early part of the nineteenth century. Employers frequently saw the workforce as a simple resource that could be exploited in return for maximum personal profits. It became clear, however, that workforces could be better motivated and more effective and efficient if some of their basic needs were catered for in terms of wages, employment contracts and a better working environment. Attempts were made to cater for the needs of the workforce at a number of different levels, including the provision of better homes, schools and medical services. The success of this approach can be seen in places such as New Lanark in Scotland, which was developed around a manufacturing plant where the employers catered for the needs of the workers. Employers began to take on greater responsibility for the lives and care of their employees over a very broad spectrum of activities, up to and including the standard of housing made available.

MANAGEMENT STYLE

According to management literature of the 1960s and 1970s, the difference between "utilitarian" and "enlightened" management is underscored by some non-academic but none the less prevalent beliefs. On the one hand, people who employ others tend to see the employing role as fundamental. The employer is the risk-taker, the entrepreneur, the captain of industry, and the workforce is consequently seen as having a duty to these risk-takers and to the shareholders who support the enterprise. Within such a philosophy, work can be viewed as a privilege. Not surprisingly, perhaps, this

4

view tends to gain impetus and media support during times of economic recession. A different perspective arises out of the central tenet that, without a workforce, nothing would be manufactured or achieved at all. From this viewpoint employers have a duty to the workforce, without which they are powerless. This second perspective gains credence in times of economic growth.

These two views of the relative roles of the employer and the employed are important, and it is worthwhile citing one of the more popular management theories of the time. McGregor *(11,12)* divided management theories into two simple categories that he called Theory X and Theory Y. According to Theory X, management is responsible for organizing the elements of productive enterprise, money, materials, equipment and people in the interest of economic ends. With respect to people this involves directing their efforts, motivating them, controlling their behaviour and modifying their actions to fit the needs of the organization. From such a viewpoint, management is strong, hard when necessary, coercive and controlling. McGregor suggested that such a theory was out of date, inefficient and unlikely to be of maximum benefit to employer or employee. He suggested a Theory Y, in which the central task of management is to arrange conditions and modes of operation so that people can achieve their own goals best by directing their efforts towards organizational objectives. The catch phrase of the time under this theory was "Management by objectives, not management by control". This is related to the ideas of Maslow *(13)* who believed that people have a need for "self-actualization". According to these "modern theories of management", the role of managers was to enable people to achieve "self-actualization" through their work.

The reactions of organizations to their employees' alcohol problems can be seen to reflect the two perspectives in management theory described above. From a Theory X standpoint, an employee whose work is impaired due to alcohol use should simply be fired and replaced by someone whose work is not so impaired. This course of action may be the most economically efficient way of dealing with the situation, at least in circumstances where the category of labour does not require a great deal of training and where there are others willing to do the work. From a Theory Y point of view, one could argue that management has a duty towards its workers, including various aspects of their health and social functioning. In this case, some attempt should be made to look after employees with alcohol-related problems rather than automatically dismissing them. Although management style is likely to affect how employees with alcohol-related problems are treated, it is not the only factor that determines this. There are a number of other considerations to be taken into account, such as legal and safety requirements.

ALCOHOL USE WITHIN THE WORKPLACE

For a variety of historical and conceptual reasons, it is apparent that the study of alcohol use within the workplace is a minefield of conflicting value judgements. It can be argued that where sensitive or complex tasks are being carried out, such as in manufacturing industries producing technologically complex machinery or carrying out tasks on which human life depends, the workforce should be sober and competent when assembling these machines or performing these duties. In situations where the safety of the public and employees is of concern, the penalties for alcohol consumption can be quite severe; in some transport-related industries, for example, a positive result to a random breath test can lead to immediate dismissal. Safety and the particular requirements of a job can therefore have a significant effect on decisions about how to treat employees who are found to be "over the limit". There are a number of costs associated with dismissing an employee, with keeping problem-drinking employees at work, and with rehabilitating and returning employees to work. Companies clearly need to consider all alternatives within an economic cost–benefit framework; if it can be shown that it makes economic sense to treat employees with drinking problems, this provides a powerful justification for doing so.

The way in which different ideas about the relative responsibilities of employers and employees apply to the specific problem of alcohol use in the workplace is further complicated by the lack of any clear definition of "alcohol misuse" or "alcoholism". Describing someone as suffering from alcoholism is, at least implicitly, to accept the disease perspective of alcohol use, a perspective that sees the individual's alcohol consumption as originating from a (usually) innate predisposition or vulnerability to drinking alcohol. From such a standpoint, the person with an alcohol problem is "sick" in much the same way as someone suffering from pneumonia, a broken limb or some other sort of incapacitation. Consequently, the employer's approach to an employee who has an alcohol-related problem should be the same as the approach made to an employee who is suffering from any other health problem. At the same time, however, it is intuitively obvious that a great many people who are not normally regarded as alcoholics can on occasion drink to the detriment of their general performance, including their work performance and social relationships. Such a person is not seen in lay terms as necessarily being an "alcoholic" but as someone who has deliberately consumed alcohol and is therefore responsible for the consequences of that excessive consumption. This is the approach generally taken within the law when a person attributes a particular act to a state of intoxication. Even if the person is not held responsible for the act, he or she may none the less be held responsible for having consumed the alcohol in the first place. Since no clear distinction exists between the two modes of consumption, policy on these matters may appear whimsical.

These two different philosophies may also be applied differentially according to the status of the employee within the organization. For example, a top manager who appears to be drunk at work may be seen as having the "disease" of alcoholism, and is treated and remains in work, whereas someone on the shop floor exhibiting a similar type of behaviour may be seen as "bad" rather than sick and consequently dismissed.

ALCOHOL POLICIES

We find, therefore, considerable variability in the way that companies deal with alcohol-related problems, a variability manifested both in the types of alcohol policies that firms and organizations have in place and also in the ways these are implemented between as well as within firms. At one extreme, we find examples of practice that involve referring problem drinkers to agencies of various kinds, the provision of continued support and the safeguarding of jobs. At the other extreme, we find examples of breathalysers in place at the entrance to the workplace (with anyone found providing a positive reading being denied access), summary dismissal for any offence involving alcohol, and restrictions placed on employees' behaviour both inside and outside the working environment. These are clearly very different approaches to solving problems associated with alcohol consumption.

There are clearly a number of ways in which alcohol-related problems can be approached. What is not clear, however, is which approaches are likely to be the most successful in particular circumstances. In the following review we describe a range of different approaches to alleviating alcohol-related problems and, where possible, assess the effectiveness of these approaches. Of particular concern is the accuracy of current estimates of "cost" and the effects that these estimates have on the perception of the seriousness of alcohol-related problems, a perception that plays a major role in motivating the introduction of alcohol control measures.

1

The Effects of Alcohol Use at Work

Alcohol can have a number of effects on a workplace, effects that have consequences for, among others, absenteeism, productivity, the accident rate, the turnover rate of employees, the "atmosphere" within the company, and the company image projected to customers. Four of the most important of these effects are discussed in detail below.

ALCOHOL-RELATED ABSENCE

Absenteeism is a major problem facing industry today. It has been estimated that in the United Kingdom, for example, 3.5–5% of working time may be lost through unauthorized and unaccounted for absences and sick leave (14). Such absences have direct implications for productivity and the profitability of companies, and are therefore of major concern to employers.

It is well documented that employees who drink heavily take more time off work than those who do not (15). This has been demonstrated in American studies of "recovered" alcoholics (16–19) and in studies of problem drinkers in employment (20,21). From this research it is estimated that problem drinkers are absent between two and eight times more than their non-problem-drinking colleagues (22,23), a relationship that has also been observed in a number of other countries including Australia, France, Sweden and the United Kingdom (24,25).

9

It is not only "problem drinking" that may be related to absence, since occasional excessive or inappropriate drinking may also increase absence as a result, for example, of hangovers or early leaving after lunchtime drinking sessions. The relationship between alcohol consumption and such absenteeism would appear to be a strong one (26). Those employees who were more likely to get drunk frequently, to drink at work and to have reported alcohol-related problems tended to take more time off work. The relationship between alcohol consumption and absenteeism is not a simple, linear relationship since it interacts with other types of behaviour such as smoking, the environment in which alcohol is consumed, and the general level of health and possibly of stress (27,28).

ACCIDENTS

Alcohol is associated with accidents primarily due to its effect on the nervous system, which leads to impairment of thinking skills, increased reaction time and reduced muscle control. These effects have obvious implications for safety and become increasingly pronounced as more alcohol enters the bloodstream. Impairments caused by alcohol use have been linked to a whole range of serious and fatal injuries, including spinal cord injuries (29), drownings (30), car accidents (31–35) and bicycle crashes (36), as well as a number of individual accidents (26,37,38).

Data on admissions to hospital casualty departments provide valuable information about the relationship between alcohol consumption and accidents, and have typically found alcohol to be implicated in 15–25% of non-fatal incidents (39–44). Goodman et al. (45) found that alcohol consumption and death by accidental injury were correlated, with higher injury rates being found for those who had higher blood alcohol levels.

The use of casualty department data also enables a number of interesting cross-cultural comparisons to be made. For example, Cherpitel (46) compared casualties admitted to hospital in countries with different drinking cultures and found evidence to support the argument that alcohol consumption increases the risk of accidents. Cherpitel et al. (47) compared data collected in Italy, where there is frequently drinking during working hours, with data collected in the United States, where alcohol consumption is normally concentrated at the weekend. Accidents in the United States tended to be concentrated at the weekend, whereas in Italy this was not the case. This study, although not proving any direct causal link between the two, at least suggests that alcohol intake is related to the number of accidents.

Surveys have also indicated that alcohol consumption may be implicated in up to 25% of industrial accidents. For example, 15–25% of industrial accidents in France are thought to be alcohol-related *(48)*, while in Poland the figure is estimated at 8–25% *(22)*; in tests over a number of years, 16% of those killed in accidents had alcohol in their blood *(49)*. In Texas it was found that 13.3% of those killed at work had measurable blood alcohol levels *(50)* and a similar figure (10.7%) was found in Alberta in Canada *(51)*. In the United Kingdom, alcohol is estimated to be implicated in 20% of accidents, a figure obtained by the Health and Safety Executive *(52)* who measured blood alcohol levels in 40% of the 92 fatal accidents reported to them in 1979–1980. Of the 35 blood alcohol estimations carried out, 7 (20%) involved levels in excess of the legal driving limit (a much higher level than the "observable" levels identified in the studies quoted above). While this figure is based on an extremely small sample, it is similar in magnitude to those from other, often much more extensive surveys. Comparing data from different countries with those from the United Kingdom may be questioned on the grounds that different countries are likely to have fundamentally different cultures and working practices, which may in some way affect the recorded accident levels. Although survey data provide an indication of the number of accidents in which alcohol *may* be implicated, they do not demonstrate any causal link *(25,33)*.

A number of studies that have used control groups also claim to support the hypothesis that alcohol consumption and accidents are related. Lederman & Metz *(53)* estimated an increase of 10–11 times in the chance of accidents among employees with raised blood alcohol levels compared to those who had not drunk any alcohol. Within problem-drinking populations, the evidence of a relationship between accidents and alcohol also appears to be strong. Maxwell *(20)* estimated that problem drinkers have 3.6 times more accidents than non-problem drinkers, while Popham et al. *(54)* found that males in their

11

study who were designated as heavy drinkers or alcohol-dependent were 2.5–8 times more likely to have an accident. In a study of "alcoholics", Eckardt et al. *(55)* found that members of this group were 5 times more likely to die in car crashes, 16 times more likely to die in falls, and 10 times more likely to become fire or burn victims. Additional evidence for the relationship between alcohol and accidents is provided by Anda et al. *(56)* who found that, from a sample of over 13 000 non-institutionalized American adults, those who drank five or more drinks per occasion[1] had a significantly higher mortality rate through injury than those drinking fewer than five drinks per occasion. Finally, in a study on absence from work, Webb et al. (unpublished data, 1992) found that 26% of problem drinkers had accidents requiring leave from work compared to only 10% of non-problem drinkers.

Accurate estimates of the relationship between alcohol consumption and workplace accidents are difficult to calculate, as the reasons for accidents often remain hidden. Employees and employers often "cover up" accidents, and many companies do not automatically test for blood alcohol after an accident. Employers often fear the implications for industrial relations and, as a result, find it easier to do nothing *(57)*. Alcohol-related accidents are likely to be underreported, a tendency that appears to be particularly pronounced in countries that have severe legal sanctions against intoxicated workers and their superiors. In Poland, for example, where surveys have indicated that alcohol is implicated in 8–25% of accidents, official figures identify only 0.5% of accidents as being related to alcohol *(58)*.

In addition to the points raised above, attempting to assess the contribution played by alcohol in causing accidents by interpreting accident rate figures is made difficult by the avoidance tactics often used by heavy drinkers. Such an effect was demonstrated in a study by Trice *(18)* who pointed out that only 18–21% of the members of Alcoholics Anonymous reported having had accidents, a figure not significantly different from the population average. Given the likely effect of alcohol on performance and the number of studies that demonstrate a positive correlation between the two, such a finding

---

[1] Anda et al. used self-reported quantity of consumption per drinking occasion, as this was shown to be a strong predictor of fatal injury.

warrants closer inspection. This result may be explained, however, by looking at the type of work conducted by problem and non-problem drinkers. Problem-drinking employees tend to reduce the chance of having accidents by avoiding high-risk situations. This results in qualitative differences in the type of work done by problem and non-problem drinkers, making valid comparisons between the groups difficult. In such circumstances the expected relationship between alcohol consumption and accident rates may not materialize. Experienced workers may also be more able to avoid dangerous situations or to organize their work patterns (or have them organized for them) to fit around their drinking behaviour. Some evidence for this has been found in Poland *(59)*, where it is often the case that heavy drinkers are transferred to safer work (often as a result of disciplinary downgrading) where their drinking habits no longer pose a threat to themselves or their colleagues.

JOB PERFORMANCE

Alcohol consumption can affect human performance in a number of ways. It has been shown, for example, to affect gross motor coordination *(60,61)*, attention *(62)* and reaction time *(61,63,64)*. Working while under the influence of alcohol is likely to result in a reduction in efficiency and accuracy at work. Tasks are likely to be completed more slowly and less accurately, which will inevitably reduce overall output at work. This tendency has been reported by problem-drinking employees who have indicated declines in their own performance *(16–18,24)*. Blum et al. *(65)* provide evidence that in a group of 136 employees, the 25% who drank the most per month scored significantly lower on a number of performance measures.

As it is difficult to calculate the overall effect that alcohol consumption has on performance, the reduction in productivity due to alcohol use can, at present, only be guessed at. However, given the demonstrable effects of alcohol consumption on performance, the production losses experienced by at least those companies where motor and thinking skills are at a premium may be substantial. A decline in work performance would appear to be an important consideration when assessing the effects of alcohol use, and could be one of the major alcohol-related costs to industry (see Chapter 2).

WORKING RELATIONS

Many of the effects that alcohol consumption has on human behaviour and emotions are well known, most notably the effect it has on interpersonal behaviour as a result of lowered inhibitions (66–69). The reduction of such inhibitions and the perceived benefits that this provides are far from unwanted side-effects of alcohol consumption, and are often identified by people as the reason for drinking. While such effects may be quite acceptable within a social setting, they have a particular relevance to the workplace. A number of studies have shown alcohol use within the workplace to be linked to both positive and negative consequences. On the one hand, it has been linked to thefts, aggression, arguments with bosses and customers, and lost promotion (70–73). It has also been found to encourage the formation of informal groups, which can be destructive in that often these groups may not reveal work-related plans to other colleagues and may thereby adversely affect production (22). On the other hand, alcohol use can help to sustain informal groups, improve relationships between managers and employees (74), help with team-building and work as a reinforcer to some extent.

2

The Economics of Alcohol Use

THE OVERALL ECONOMIC IMPACT OF THE ALCOHOL INDUSTRY

The scale and importance of the alcohol industry can be gauged to some extent through estimates of, for example, the number of people who regularly drink alcohol, the economic "value" of the industry, and the number of people employed in the production, distribution and selling of alcoholic products (75). The worldwide popularity of alcohol is indicated by estimates showing that a large percentage of the adult population drink, at least occasionally. A survey conducted in the United Kingdom in 1984 showed that 94% of men and 90% of women drank alcohol at least occasionally. Perhaps more revealing of the extent of British drinking are figures obtained from a study showing that 75% of men and 56% of women had consumed alcohol in the seven days preceding an interview (76,77). Although it is difficult to compare such figures, it is clear that alcoholic drinks are immensely popular and that there is a substantial worldwide market.

According to a report published by the Amsterdam Group (4) the market in alcoholic drinks in the European Community (EC) in 1990 was estimated to be worth some ECU 127 billion[2] (ECU 389 per head), which amounted to around 2.6% of total consumer spending within the Community. This had consequences for the EC's balance of trade, as the value of alcohol exports was greater than that of imports. This led to a trade surplus of ECU 5.6 billion for the

---

[2] 1 billion = 10^9.

import/export of alcohol, and helped to offset the EC's overall deficit on all merchandise of ECU 42.9 billion for the same year.

The number of people worldwide who gain a livelihood from the alcohol beverage industry is substantial but cannot be easily calculated. There are no readily available figures for the numbers involved in the production, distribution and sale of alcoholic drinks, although there is some information from 1965 on the production of beer and spirits (78–80). Estimating the importance of the alcohol industry is also difficult, as there is some dispute over whether to classify as profits some of the commonly quoted "gains", in particular the creation of new workplaces and income from alcohol taxation (22,81).

ESTIMATES OF THE COST OF ALCOHOL USE

An important consideration in determining the overall economic effect of the alcohol industry is the costs and benefits commonly associated with alcohol consumption. Although it is very hard to incorporate such information into any single index of overall benefit or cost, some estimates of the cost associated with alcohol use have been made for a number of countries, as shown in Table 1. Although similar statistics are provided, these estimates cannot be regarded as comparable as they have been calculated using a variety of methodologies, involve data that are variable in quality (6) and are often based on different constituent costs. While these estimates can provide only a rough indication of the scale of costs that *might* be associated with alcohol use, they are of particular interest in that they indicate the importance attributed to alcohol use within these countries.

It can be argued that many of the estimates of costs shown in Table 1 may be low owing to a number of important factors not being considered. For example, a number of estimates do not include costs associated with accidents, lost output, poor working relations and mistakes attributable to alcohol use (see Chapter 1). It can also be argued, however, that estimates may be rather high, as a number of costs are often included that may not actually be costs in any real

Table 1. Estimates of the annual cost of alcohol problems[a]

Country	Source	Cost	Percentage of GNP
Australia	Collins & Lapsley (82) (see Richmond et al. (83))	A $6.23 billion	–
Finland	Kasurinen (84)	FM 2 billion	1.5
Georgia	Moser (6)	R 0.21 billion	–
Germany	Kieselbach (85) (see ILO (86))	DM 80–120 billion	–
New Zealand	Chetwynd & Rayner (87)	NZ $0.58 billion	2.3
Poland	Hansen (88)	–	2.0
Spain	Moser (6)	Ptas 43 billion	–
Sweden	Moser (6)	Skr 5 billion	–
Former USSR	Morawski et al. (22)	–	10
United Kingdom	Holterman & Burchell (89)	£0.33 billion	–
	Maynard et al. (90)	£1.85 billion	–
	Jackson (91)	£0.9 billion	–
	Maynard (92)	£1.99 billion	–
United States	Berry & Boland (93)	US $31.4 billion	–
	Rice et al. (94)	US $70.3 billion (1985)	–
		US $85.8 billion (1988)[b]	–
	Harwood et al. (95)	US $116.9 billion	
	Burke (96)	US $136 billion[b]	

[a] Only the data provided in the source documents have been included. Calculating the percentage of GNP for all countries would be possible, but these would not be directly comparable and would thus be misleading.

[b] Projected estimate.

Source: Hutcheson et al. (28).

economic sense (28). Regardless of their validity such figures are important, however, as they provide an impetus to industry and government to reduce the overall level of inappropriate drinking at the workplace.

COSTS AND BENEFITS ASSOCIATED WITH ALCOHOL CONSUMPTION

There are a number of ways in which alcohol consumption affects industry, either directly through its effects on absence rates, accidents and interpersonal relationships within a company, or indirectly through taxes and insurance premiums. Below are set out some of the costs and benefits that have commonly been associated with alcohol consumption, and which form the basis of many of the estimates provided in Table 1.

Mortality

Alcohol-related deaths incur a number of "costs" to a company, costs mostly associated with the resources needed to recruit and train replacement workers. The ultimate cost of mortality to a company depends on the scarcity of the supply of suitable labour and the specificity of the skills of the employee. Estimates of cost are, however, usually based on the overall earning potential of the employee, a measure that has more relevance to the country as a whole than to any individual company. The loss of years of working life for people who die early as a result of excess alcohol consumption is used to estimate the loss of earnings caused by the premature deaths. While this measure provides an indication of the loss of a potential labour resource, it does not indicate the true cost to the company or indeed to the economy. This is particularly true when there is not full employment, as the employee can often be replaced by drawing on someone who was previously unemployed. The calculated loss of earnings may give the impression of a comparable loss to industry, even though this is often not the case.

Estimated costs associated with mortality may also be questioned, as there are a number of methodological problems that make accurate estimates very difficult to make. The most serious of these are the reluctance of many physicians to attribute deaths to "alcoholism" or to "alcoholic psychosis" and, more fundamentally, the lack of agreement on a definition of these terms (97). Without an agreed definition and procedure for identifying "alcoholics" there can be no consistency between studies, making them unsuitable for comparative research (98). This lack of consistency can be demonstrated in estimates of the number of alcohol-related premature deaths in the

United Kingdom, which range from 4000 to 40 000 *(90,99)* depending on the definitions used.[3]

Even though there are many methodological and theoretical problems with calculating the economic impact of alcohol-related mortality, such costs are often estimated as some of the most substantial of those associated with alcohol. Most if not all estimates are, however, very contentious and open to dispute.

Morbidity

Morbidity costs are those associated with illness, particularly with hospital admission. Although these are predominantly indirect costs to companies, they are included here as they often form a substantial proportion of the costs commonly associated with alcohol. For example, it has been estimated that in the United Kingdom up to 20% of admissions to hospital may be alcohol-related *(102,103)* with associated inpatient costs estimated to be between £88 million and £530 million in 1987 *(90,104)*. Although these did not include accident and emergency costs (estimated at £18–25 million in 1987) *(105)*, costs associated with outpatient care *(106)* or costs associated with non-statutory treatment and preventive services *(107)*, Godfrey & Maynard *(99)* conclude that alcohol use in the United Kingdom is associated with substantial amounts of current National Health Service resources.

Morbidity costs have also been calculated for a number of other countries, and indications are that such costs may be substantial. In France, for example, it was estimated that 2.8% of all cases treated in public hospitals had a principal diagnosis of alcoholism, alcoholic psychosis or cirrhosis *(108)*, 20–30% of all general hospital admissions for men and 5–10% for women were for alcohol-related problems, and 34% of male and 8% of female admissions to psychiatric hospitals were for alcoholic psychosis *(109)*. In Sweden, excessive users of alcohol in a group of men aged between 50 and 60 years were found to have incurred relatively high morbidity costs. Within that group, the 12% of men who were excessive alcohol users accounted for 40% of hospital admissions, two thirds of care and treatment for

---

[3] Most costing studies take estimates of mortality rates that lie at the lower end of this range *(100)* and are based on studies of "known alcoholics" *(101)*.

mental illness, and nearly half of all care for gastrointestinal disorders *(110)*. In Switzerland, alcohol-related problems comprise the largest group of admissions to hospital among male patients of working age, and in 1985 "alcoholism" was quoted as the second most frequent reason for admission of men to psychiatric hospital *(111)*. In the United States, the prevalence of alcohol-related disorders among hospital patients was estimated at between 3.6% and 22.4% depending on the method of assessment used *(112,113)*.

In addition to alcohol-related hospital admissions and outpatient costs, alcohol use can result in a number of other indirect costs, including those incurred through birth defects *(114–119)* and diseases transmitted as a result of high-risk sexual behaviour that may be related to alcohol use *(68,120–123)*. Such costs may be substantial, but are particularly difficult to calculate with any degree of accuracy *(124)* and are rarely included in estimates of the overall costs associated with alcohol.

Although the calculation of costs associated with morbidity can provide an indication of the burden on health services (at least the burden attributable to a few identified illnesses), they are not ideal measures for estimating the extent of a country's alcohol problem nor do they permit a comparison of data from different countries, as these measures are to some extent tied to current medical practices.

> Whilst the estimates are not precise the conclusion that alcohol is associated with substantial amounts of current NHS resource use is obvious. However, even if these estimates were improved it is not clear that it would make an appropriate indicator or outcome measure. Levels of expenditure or morbidity measures such as bed-days reflect current medical practices and are process rather than outcome measures. More effective alcohol strategies may in the short term increase expenditure because there is more accurate identification of alcohol-related health problems and more referrals for alcohol-related treatment or prevention programmes *(99)*.

Although a great deal of data relating to morbidity costs has been collected over a number of years and for many different countries, methodological problems and variability make such estimates virtually worthless and only really useful for providing approximate figures. For example, estimates for alcohol-related inpatient costs in the United Kingdom for 1987 vary from £88 million to £530 million *(104)* and estimates for the prevalence of alcohol-related disorders among hospital patients in the United States vary from 3.6% to 22.4%. Even though an accurate cost cannot be calculated on the evidence available, given the relationship between hospital admission and alcohol consumption alone even cautious estimates indicate that the costs associated with morbidity are likely to be substantial.

Social Costs

The social costs dealt with in this section are those that are alcohol-related but not borne by any one particular company. The major estimated costs are, among others, those related to unemployment, road traffic accidents and the criminal justice administration.

It has been shown that there are higher rates of unemployment among those with severe alcohol problems, which can incur significant costs for industry through, for instance, redundancy payments, retraining and legal costs. Although such costs are often estimated to be substantial, it is unclear in many cases where these costs are realized and if they are actual costs at all. For example, McDonnell & Maynard *(125)* estimated the "opportunity costs" associated with unemployment caused by alcohol use (that is, the potential earnings of the employee). This does not, however, appear to be an appropriate measure in an economy where there is less than full employment, as is currently the case in the United Kingdom.[4]

> ... it is assumed that alcohol use that produces unemployment is a cost. This may be correct in an economy where there is full employment: alcohol reduces employment, production and the size of the gross national product (GNP). However in an economy where there is unemployment, alcohol misuse leads to the alcohol misuser being replaced by a previously unemployed person. Whilst there may be costs associated with the shedding and replacement of the alcohol abusing worker, there are no significant longer term effects on employment, production and GNP *(90)*.

---

[4] Although Maynard and his colleagues make this clear, and provide an estimate for the costs associated with alcohol use that does not include unemployment, the higher figure that includes this cost is invariably the one quoted.

Other alcohol-related social costs have been estimated in the United Kingdom including, most notably, road traffic accidents (£113 million) *(104)* and alcohol-related court cases (£18.4 million at 1985 prices) *(90)*. The social costs of alcohol use in the United Kingdom and Europe as a whole are varied and often difficult to quantify, but have been identified as substantial and are likely to incur significant costs to industry.

Absenteeism

Absenteeism can incur a number of costs to industry, mostly as a result of reduced output due to days off, late reporting for work, early leaving and unscheduled breaks. Although the following section discusses alcohol-related absenteeism mostly in respect of British industry, the conclusions will be of interest for most other industrial countries.

The costs associated with alcohol-induced absenteeism in the United Kingdom have been estimated by McDonnell & Maynard *(125)* at £799.3 million and by Godfrey & Hardman *(104)* at £774 million. Such estimates are brought into question, however, by Joeman *(27)* who, on the basis of data from the General Household Survey, concluded that there were no direct reliable differences in rates of absence between light, moderate and heavy drinkers. Joeman found that a relationship between absence and drinking behaviour became apparent only when general health and smoking were taken into account. The role of alcohol consumption in determining absence rates is complex, and the number of absences that can be attributed to alcohol is uncertain. The costs associated with alcohol-related absences are, therefore, also uncertain.

Even if it were possible to derive the number of working days lost through alcohol use[5] it would still be difficult to estimate the cost to the company that this entails, as there are a number of problems

---

[5] The problems associated with estimating the amount of sick leave caused by alcohol are well documented *(89,100)*, particularly those associated with the use of company sickness certificates, which are often the only source of information as to why employees were absent. As alcohol misuse is seldom given as the reason for any time off by employees, much of the sickness data collected by companies is of little use in identifying alcohol-related absences.

with evaluating the value of the lost output. For example, an employee taking time off work may incur substantial losses for the company (as in the case of a crane driver, whose absence can stop work on an entire building site) or may incur relatively insignificant losses (for example, when other people in the company are able to cover for the employee who is away). It is no easy matter to assess the "losses" caused by each absence. Even so, some calculations have been made on the basis of employees' gross earnings and other employers' costs. While such a method produces a figure for the cost of absenteeism, it cannot claim to be an accurate reflection of the true cost to the company. Calculating the lost output in this manner might also be misleading, as employees often make up for any time lost. For example, Majewska *(126)* found that many alcoholic workers under treatment caught up on the time they missed through longer working days and the forfeit of their holiday entitlement on the basis of agreements with their supervisors.

In the present working environment it can be argued that absenteeism should not necessarily be included as a cost in the same way that accidents and job performance detriments can be. Martin et al. *(25)* make the point that:

> ... substance abusers' absenteeism reflected efforts to protect themselves from harm that might occur if they tried to work; obviously this protection can extend to co-workers and to the workplace itself. While seeming absurd, the suggestion that absenteeism can serve positive functions stands in the face of very imperfect systems of detection of employed substance abusers or implementing effective means for their behavioral change.

Absences from work due to alcohol might therefore be seen as having some beneficial consequences. In a workforce with a developed drinking culture, for example, absenteeism can serve the positive goal of reducing accidents and poor performance through alcohol use. If alcohol problems cannot be eliminated entirely from a workforce, it could be beneficial for companies to accommodate their employees' drinking habits by making time off work easier to obtain (maybe in conjunction with stricter penalties for those who arrive at work under the influence of alcohol) as such a strategy might reduce costs associated with reduced production and accidents.

Absenteeism is regarded as one of the major costs to industry arising from alcohol use. Estimates of the actual costs involved are, however, open to dispute as there are a number of difficulties in estimating the amount of time "lost" and the value of the "lost" production. Accurate estimates will require more detailed information about the causes of absences and, when assessing the associated costs, individual agreements between employees and employers about making up for lost time must be taken into account.[6]

Accidents

One of the most highly publicized and prominent concerns regarding alcohol and the workplace is its relationship with accidents. There have been a number of high-profile cases where alcohol consumption has been implicated in accidents, particularly those involving transportation. Two of the more costly incidents were a railway crash in Louisiana that resulted in US $16 million of damage and the Exxon Valdez oil tanker, which ran aground in Alaska and caused catastrophic environmental and economic damage (26). Although it cannot be proved that alcohol was indeed to blame for these accidents, it was at least one of the factors that may have been responsible. While such examples can involve substantial costs, they are isolated incidents and do not provide much of an indication of the day-to-day costs of accidents within companies.

To provide some indication of the *possible* losses that may be incurred as a result of more common accidents, the Health and Safety Executive (127) conducted a study in five different companies. In this study, costs associated with accidents were calculated, with an accident being defined broadly as "any unplanned event that results in injury or ill health of people, or damage or loss of property, plant, materials or the environment or a loss of business opportunity". The losses estimated in this study are shown in Table 2.

It should be noted that these estimates do not include any "catastrophic" or major losses, as there were no examples of these during the period of study. Even so, the costs of accidental loss were

---

[6] This practice might be quite prevalent, particularly in smaller companies.

Table 2. Financial losses due to accidents in five British companies,
1990–1991

Company	Total loss	Representing
Construction site	£700 000	8.5% of tender price
Creamery	£975 336	1.4% of operating costs
Transport company	£195 712	1.8% of operating costs and 37% of profits
Oil platform	£3 763 684	14.2% of potential output
Hospital	£397 140	5% of annual running costs

Source: Health and Safety Executive (127).

regarded by management as significant, with large amounts of money involved representing substantial proportions of operating costs and profits. According to the Office of Population Censuses and Surveys (128), in the United Kingdom each year there are around 1.6 million accidents resulting in injury, contributing to the estimated £4–9 billion overall cost to industry of accidents and work-related ill health (127,129). The total cost of accidents and work-related ill health to society as a whole is substantially higher and is estimated at £10–15 billion a year.

The findings from a number of studies show that alcohol consumption is likely to be related to accidents both within and outside the workplace. The precise relationship is poorly understood and precludes any accurate assessment of the precise role played by alcohol consumption in *causing* accidents, and any estimation of the likely cost.

Job Performance

Estimating the extent and cost of reduction in performance due to alcohol consumption is not straightforward (see Chapter 1) but some estimates have nevertheless been made. One of the more widely used methods for estimating the value of lost output is the Stanford Model. According to this method, an "average alcoholic" works at only 75% efficiency (87,130), which is assumed to result in 25% of salary costs being lost. For a company as a whole, the cost of alcohol use is calculated by multiplying the proportion of the workforce considered to have a severe alcohol problem by their reduction in performance. In a country where it is estimated that 5% of employees have a severe alcohol problem, the overall cost of lost production is calculated as 1.25% of the total wage and salary costs. There are, however, problems with calculating lost output costs on the basis of salary costs. There are many more costs associated with employing people than wages, pensions, heating and lighting and security, for example.

The accuracy of this equation also rests on a number of estimates that cannot be regarded as reliable, such as assessing the number of employees who may be regarded as having a severe alcohol problem and the degree to which this affects their overall performance. The equation is also limited as a method for estimating overall lost output, as it does not take into account production losses associated with non-problem drinkers who, because of their greater numbers, may pose an even larger threat to production than problem drinkers *(131)*.

Turnover

Turnover of employees, either between companies or between different jobs in the same company, is a cost to industry in that new employees have to be recruited and trained. Alcohol consumption has often been implicated in increased turnover rates, but the precise nature of the relationship is unclear. Schollaert *(132)* found that, in a study of 161 employed alcoholics, 36% had changed jobs during the five years before starting treatment. Schollaert did not, however, provide turnover rates for non-alcoholics, which reduces the value of the study, but did show that variables describing drinking behaviour appeared to be central to the turnover process. Direct evidence for a link between alcohol consumption and changing jobs within a company is provided by Morawski *(59)* who showed that problem drinkers in Poland change their position within a plant significantly more than non-problem drinkers. This effect was partly due to the transfer of individuals with alcohol-related problems to less exacting or less dangerous jobs *within* a company; it also resulted in less turnover of staff *between* companies as the employees could still function, albeit in a lower position, and remain working at the plant *(25)*.

Working Relations

Alcohol consumption at work can cause a number of problems, many of which have been outlined in Chapter 1. The costs involved are difficult to quantify and have rarely been included in overall estimates of the costs of alcohol use. It should also be noted that alcohol consumption can serve some positive purpose at the workplace, and could even have positive economic consequences for companies. For example, alcohol consumption by managers appears to play an important role in the relationship between themselves and their staff, a relationship that has a number of consequences for working relationships and possibly also for productivity. Alcohol consumption by employees may also have some beneficial consequences in that it can improve social relationships and team-building, both of which can have positive economic benefits.

Alcohol can also serve to reinforce the workforce, a role most commonly seen in company parties arranged as a reward for reaching production targets or securing new contracts. In addition to these occasions, many companies hold regular office parties that serve a similar function and are seen to promote better relations between employees. Although alcohol should not be seen as essential to the celebration (which can be viewed as the major reinforcer) it does often play an important role. The beneficial effects of such staff gatherings are extremely difficult to quantify in economic terms, and such effects have thus rarely been taken into account when the cost of alcohol consumption is calculated. The importance of celebrations and, it can be argued, alcohol, can be gauged by the reluctance of many employers to ban alcohol from such occasions. Celebrations are considered to be very important in looking after the workforce, and alcohol is often viewed as an important component of such celebrations.[7]

Although the effects that alcohol has on personal relationships are often dramatic and obvious, the precise effect it exerts on overall productivity is much harder to quantify. Many of the effects of alcohol consumption, at least when it is consumed in small quantities,

---

[7] Acceptance of the use of alcohol (or even the encouragement of its use) in certain circumstances by management may lead to some benefits, but may also make it difficult to promote an alcohol-free workplace (see Chapter 5).

are quite subtle. For this reason it is not possible at the present time to estimate the gains and losses incurred through the effect that alcohol consumption in the workplace has on working relations.

3

Factors Related to Alcohol Consumption at the Workplace

As many policies focus on identifying employees with drinking problems, the contribution played by the workplace in encouraging and maintaining this behaviour is often overlooked. This is unfortunate, as workplace factors can have a major effect on drinking patterns and overall levels of consumption. Of particular concern is the relationship between overall levels of drinking and particular working environments, how consumption might relate to the type of work conducted, and the role played by "normal and accepted" working practices in encouraging and maintaining drinking behaviour.

WORKSITE-SPECIFIC FACTORS

The level of drinking at a particular workplace may partly depend on the type of working environment that exists within a company. This environment can exert a powerful influence on the creation and maintenance of drinking cultures through factors such as the accessibility of alcohol and the ease with which it may be consumed on company premises. Cooper & Sadri (133) recognize the importance of the working environment and have gone so far as to argue that a work environment characterized by general excessive alcohol consumption is more a condemnation of the working conditions themselves than a reflection on the people who consume the alcohol. A heavy-drinking workforce may therefore be, according to these authors, a symptom of a "sick" working environment. Overall alcohol consumption may be reduced by changing drinking habits and creating "alcohol-unfriendly" workplaces. Some steps that have been suggested to this end are to make alcohol-free drinks readily available, not to offer alcoholic drinks in company canteens, to offer subsidized food and soft drinks to discourage lunchtime trips to the local pub, to make rest rooms "un-publike" by restricting smoking and making them bright, clean and open, and to identify places that may be used by employees who secretly drink (134,135). It is particularly important for management to set an example by, for instance, banning alcohol from the board room and removing private bars in offices. Such action will help to change drinking habits within a company, and also make it harder for employees to drink at work.

Policies in the United States have emphasized the provision of treatment for employees with alcohol-related problems to the near exclusion of rules regarding the availability of alcohol at work and drinking for the ordinary employee (136). According to Ames et al. (137) this constitutes a serious fault in the way policies are run in the United States and may help account for the apparent lack of success in reducing the overall occurrence of drinking problems at work (138). There is evidence that a similar situation exists elsewhere, as many companies view their alcohol policies as solely relating to the problem drinker and not to those who occasionally drink inappropriately. Companies may therefore make no attempt, as part of alcohol policy, to change the underlying reasons for employees drinking.

JOB-SPECIFIC FACTORS

In addition to the work environment, the type of job may exert a strong influence on the amount of alcohol an employee is likely to drink. Based on evidence of differential mortality rates from liver cirrhosis among men in different occupations, those in particular occupations are especially vulnerable to alcohol-related problems (128,139–141). The main factors suggested to explain this increased vulnerability are the availability of alcohol at work (134), social pressure to drink, lack of job flexibility or repetitive tasks leading to boredom (142), separation from normal social or sexual relationships, low levels of supervision, lack of visibility of work (143,144), and particularly high or low income levels.

While such factors may have a powerful effect on the level of drinking, it should be noted that certain occupations might attract heavy drinkers, as such posts allow them to continue drinking while they are at work. The type of work conducted may not in itself, therefore, be entirely responsible for the high drinking levels. In such circumstances it might prove beneficial for a company that is concerned about the level of drinking among its prospective employees to operate pre-employment screening – an option already used to some effect in the United States. In addition to screening potential employees for an existing alcohol problem, companies can reduce the effect that factors associated with excess drinking may have by, for example, reducing time away from home through changed work schedules and introducing a greater variety of work.

THE EFFECT OF "NORMAL" WORKING PRACTICES

In addition to the effects that the working environment and the type of job can have on the level of drinking at work, the attitudes of employees to drinking and the "normal" working practices that exist also exert a powerful influence on employee behaviour and can, in some situations at least, be more influential than company rules about alcohol consumption.

> ... there may be a formal policy about drinking mandated by upper management that is all but ignored by the majority of employees, who are responding to less socially distant behavioural expectations that make alcohol use appropriate – even desirable – under some circumstances. ... For example, while drinking on the job in a construction company may be against company policy, it may be understood by groups of bricklayers, painters, or carpenters that Friday afternoons are a time for 'taking it easy' and 'having a few beers'. Similar drinking behaviour in another occupational group, computer programmers for example, may result in disciplinary action or dismissal *(145)*.

The company policy on alcohol consumption at work may therefore be totally ignored by the construction workers, who are responding to the more immediate and powerful understanding that drinking on a Friday afternoon occurs and is acceptable. Once the consumption of alcohol has become embedded in work and work-related activities, enforcing policies to prohibit drinking can become costly and disruptive.

It is important to note, however, that not all drinking "norms" that appear in contravention of alcohol policies are bad for the company. Some of these norms have developed precisely because they serve the immediate needs of the company and the individual worker. For example, drinking networks may carry symbolic or actual functions important to the goals of the work organization. These may include soothing the burden of long shift-work routines and facilitating social team-building (146). Such "beneficial" practices are difficult to change, and policies that appear to interfere with them are likely to meet stiff resistance from all levels of the workforce. The tacit acceptance of certain drinking cultures serves to dilute any policy and makes the establishment of an alcohol-free workplace much harder to achieve.

Given the importance of these norms in determining workplace drinking practices, an alcohol policy may be more successful if it addresses these issues. The minor impact that alcohol policies appear to have had on the overall level of drinking in the United States (147) may be due to the low priority accorded to the *workplace* in prevention and intervention efforts (138). One of the pressing problems facing researchers in the alcohol field is the identification of the powerful forces that operate within the workplace and how these can influence drinking behaviour.

4

Workplace Alcohol Policies

POLICY CONSTRUCTION

An effective policy must be constructed specifically for the company in which it is to be used, and with the participation of all key staff. Policy-makers must recognize that each company is different and that no one policy will be effective for all companies.

The degree to which alcohol use at a particular workplace is restricted, for example, depends very much on the company, the type of work conducted and the importance of promoting the required corporate image. These factors can lead to very different policies as the two extracts below demonstrate, the first from Kent County Council in England and the second from Heathrow Airport Ltd, London.

Moderate drinking of alcohol is acceptable. It is equally acceptable for people not to drink alcohol at all if they do not wish to.

Staff will not be permitted to drink alcohol whilst on duty under any circumstances. This policy will also apply to low alcohol or 'alcohol-free' drinks as staff should understand that the smell of alcohol on the breath may cause offence. ... Staff must not use any bars on or off the airport whilst on duty, even for the consumption of non-alcoholic drinks. This includes lunch periods or official rest breaks. ... Staff in uniform or protective clothing, who could be identified as HAL employees, must not use any bar dispensing alcohol either on or off airport.

It is imperative that the key personnel who are to be involved in its preparation, implementation and evaluation are convinced of the need for a policy. This will often require an operational analysis of the company and scrutiny of a number of areas that may be affected by alcohol, such as absence and accident rates. Numerous articles have been written outlining the way in which policies may be constructed to meet specific company requirements *(134,135,148)* and this issue will not be discussed in any great detail here.

EXAMPLES OF ALCOHOL POLICIES

Boxes 1–7 provide examples of alcohol policies currently being used in different types of company in Europe. The information provided was collected during interviews with company personnel and from copies of alcohol policies that the companies provided.

EVALUATION OF ALCOHOL POLICIES

A vital but often overlooked component of a policy is that of evaluation. This is important as it provides information about the policy's effectiveness, enables the economic consequences to be evaluated and maintains awareness of the issues. The Health Education Authority in England *(148)* states that:

> Evaluation should be seen as an integral part of the introduction of an alcohol policy within the workplace ... any policy not subject to continuous monitoring, assessment and evaluation risks becoming obsolete.

Effective evaluation may also be essential for the continuing provision of health promotion, as departments are increasingly being asked to provide a "value-for-money" service. Unfortunately, it appears that the evaluation of health services within companies is relatively poor, as has been demonstrated in a recent survey conducted by the Confederation of British Industry (CBI) *(14)*:

> ... more and more emphasis is being placed on the ability of providers within companies to offer a 'value for money' service ... Forty percent of respondents to CBI's survey were able to quantify the cost of the

occupational health services they provide. The average expenditure was £415 000 per year, with 10% of these respondents spending more than £1 million annually. However, of the companies able to quantify this expenditure, only 11% were able to assess whether the service they provide is cost effective.

Examples of Evaluations

As evaluations of the effects of occupational health services and policies in Europe are rare, we have to look to studies conducted in the United States for information on the effectiveness of alcohol and general health policies. For instance, Blose & Holder *(149)*, in a study of company health care costs following the introduction of a policy, examined the records of more than 2200 insured workers over a 14-year period. The study concluded that treatment for alcohol-related problems led to a decrease in health care costs, but that the benefits were related to age. Following treatment, health care costs declined for those under 50 years of age but not for those aged over 50 years. This finding highlights the importance of early detection and treatment of problems – the older the employee, the less cost-effective the treatment.

Holder & Blose *(150)* also assessed the effects of treatment for "alcoholism" on a company's overall health care costs. More than 3000 records from treated alcoholics belonging to a single health plan, collected over a 14-year period, were assessed. Two designs were used to address aspects of validity while assessing cost changes. The first method used a pre- and post-treatment design as well as an untreated control group. This revealed, on average, a 23% general decline in health care costs following treatment. The second method used a time-series design over a 14-year period and revealed that the health care costs of treated alcoholics were 24% lower than those of untreated alcoholics. This study demonstrated the long-term beneficial effects that treatment can provide, and gives some support to estimates that for every dollar spent by an American company on a workplace policy the return is between 2 and 7 dollars.

Box 1. Example of an alcohol policy in a transport company

Number of employees: 300

Pertinent issues: New legislation
Random/with cause testing for alcohol and drugs
Employee and passenger safety
Liability to prosecution

Policy introduced: Pre-1982

Outline of policy

Aims
- To alert employees to the risks of heavy drinking.
- To assist employees who suspect they have an alcohol-related problem voluntarily to seek help from helping agencies at an early stage.
- To refer employees to helping agencies during disciplinary procedures thought to arise from an alcohol problem.

Theory and definitions
- Alcohol-related problems are seen as primarily a health and social concern.
- An alcohol-related problem is defined as drinking that interferes with an employee's health and social functioning and/or work capability or conduct.

Procedures
- Publicity ensures that employees are aware of the problems.
- No alcohol may be consumed on-site (or even off-site when in uniform).
- Employees are offered the opportunity to seek diagnosis and treatment both in disciplinary cases and in cases of voluntary referral. Treatment is arranged by the Employee Counselling Service (ECS).
- The ECS informs Personnel only if absence from work is likely, and sick leave is granted if necessary.
- Further opportunities offered in the event of a recurrence of the problem after treatment.
- Random excessive indulgence is *not* covered by the policy.
- Confidentiality of employee records is strictly preserved.
- The policy applies to *all* employees, irrespective of the position held.
- The policy cover extends to gambling and solvent abuse.

Box 2. Example of an alcohol policy at an airport

Number of employees: About 1200

Pertinent issues: Safety and security
Policy being reviewed and updated to include all employees
Strong unions

Policy introduced: First draft April 1991 – currently under review

Outline of policy

Aims
- To enable employees to obtain skilled help and advice.
- To restore the performance and capability of any staff member with a drinking problem to an acceptable level within a reasonable time.

Theory and definitions
- Alcohol depresses parts of the brain normally controlling the social and personal rules of behaviour.
- Alcohol causes the loss of up to 14 million working days per year.
- Alcohol abuse should be treated as an illness, and as such the individual concerned should be treated as would any individual suffering a period of sickness.

Procedures
- Drinking is banned on the premises and for anyone in uniform.
- It is inappropriate to resort to disciplinary measures in cases where an individual's actions can be put down to chronic alcoholism.
- Self-referral is to the medical centre, where treatment, counselling and advice can be obtained.
- Referral can also be made by the Human Resources Manager, usually in response to high absence rates. Refusal to undergo treatment, or relapse, will lead to disciplinary procedures or retirement due to ill health.
- Individuals have the right to union representation at any meetings, and the right to challenge medical reports.

Note
There is no educational element to the policy.

Box 3. Example of an alcohol policy in a health care facility

Number of employees:	2060
Pertinent issues:	Staff are in close contact with the public on a day-to-day basis
	The nature of the business means that health issues for employees are especially relevant
Policy introduced:	"A good while ago"

Outline of policy

Aims

- To alert employees to the risks associated with alcohol, drug and solvent abuse.
- To encourage employees who suspect they have a dependency problem to seek help directly or via the appropriate procedures.
- In the course of any disciplinary procedure, to offer to refer employees to an appropriate helping agency for diagnosis and, if necessary, treatment.

Theory and definitions

- Alcohol and drug dependency problems are primarily areas of health and social concern, and therefore people with such problems should have access to treatment and help.
- Alcohol dependency is defined as the consumption of alcohol, either intermittently or continually, that definitely and repeatedly interferes with a person's health, social functioning and work capability or conduct.

Procedures

- Publicity ensures that employees are aware of the problems.
- No alcohol is permitted on the premises.
- Identification of a problem can be made through voluntary referral or through referral by management.
- In cases of voluntary referral the occupational health physician will arrange appropriate help and treatment through a voluntary or statutory agency, and identify aspects of continuing support that may be required. Personnel will be informed if it is felt that the problem will affect safety or work effectiveness, and disciplinary procedures may commence.
- Referral by management will first involve an interview in the presence of a union representative. Acceptance of referral leads to an interview with Personnel staff and then to the occupational health procedure described above. Rejection of referral leads directly to disciplinary action.

Box 4. Example of an alcohol policy in the food production industry

Number of employees: 750

Pertinent issues: Policy currently being introduced after one or two alcohol-related incidents
Safety (i.e. fork-lift truck drivers)

Policy introduced: Draft currently under review

Outline of policy

Theory and definitions
- Alcohol abuse is defined as consumption of alcohol to such an extent that it affects work performance.
- Poor performance at work due to alcohol is an offence under current legislation.

Procedures
- There is a pre-employment questionnaire on alcohol use.
- Both management and employees receive education on the health risks of alcohol (awareness campaigns to be run by the Occupational Health Department).
- Management is trained to recognize "alcohol-related signs".
- Alcohol abuse is considered a disciplinary matter, but disciplinary action will be deferred to allow the employee time to seek appropriate guidance and treatment.
- A register of local alcohol support agencies is to be maintained in order to be able to refer employees as necessary.

Box 5. Example of an alcohol policy in an insurance company

Number of employees: 12 000

Pertinent issues: Employees paid weekly (on a Thursday) – lunchtime drinking culture
Possibility of a policy being drafted in 1995, and of testing being introduced

No policy–outline of procedure

Theory and definitions
- Distinction is made between abuse of alcohol for enjoyment (a disciplinary matter) and that which arises out of an alcohol problem (a capability matter).

Procedures
- No drinking is permitted on the premises as a rule (exceptions include Christmas lunch, etc.).
- It is a disciplinary offence to be under the influence of alcohol to the extent that duties and responsibilities cannot be performed, and employees are informed of this in a disciplinary handbook.
- Particular reference is made to the maintenance department.
- Assistance (through the local health authority) is given in cases where an alcohol problem exists and is admitted, and discipline will be suspended until the outcome of treatment can be evaluated.

Box 6. Example of an alcohol policy in the television industry

Number of employees: 220

Pertinent issues: Safety (i.e. drivers)
Lunchtime drinking culture
Meetings conducted in public houses (for
example by journalists)

Policy introduced: About 1984

Outline of policy

Theory and definitions

- Alcohol abuse is defined as a continuous or recurrent level of alcohol use that causes physical, psychological or social dependence leading to or resulting in a deterioration in work performance and/or the health of the individual.
- The company recognizes alcohol abuse as primarily a health problem and is therefore prepared to help people who need treatment in the same way as people who are ill, rather than regard such abuse as purely a disciplinary matter.

Procedures

- Education and awareness campaigns are conducted on alcohol-related issues.
- No alcohol is permitted on the premises.
- Voluntary or involuntary referral is to Personnel, who will put employees in touch with a professional counsellor (from an agency outside the company).
- Sick leave will be granted if absence from work is a necessary part of treatment.
- The Occupational Health Department will monitor progress during treatment.
- A union representative can be present at any stage in the procedure.
- No disciplinary action will be taken if an employee agrees to undertake counselling, unless the course of treatment is discontinued or not satisfactorily completed.
- Cases of relapse after treatment will be considered on their merits, and further opportunity for remedial action may be offered if appropriate.

Note
Nobody has yet undergone the entire procedure described above.

Box 7. Example of an alcohol policy in the theatre

Number of employees:	54 full-time and up to 150 short-term and part-time contracts
Pertinent issues:	Very varied staffing Drinking culture among staff and especially among performers Staff deal closely with the public Safety (i.e. technical staff) Alcohol present on premises

No policy—outline of procedure

Note
Ostensibly inherited a policy in March 1993; only informally adopted and still under review.

Theory and definitions
- None.

Procedures
- With the lack of an official alcohol policy things are done "more or less by word of mouth and judgement".
- People are informed of what is expected of them at interviews.
- There is no ban on alcohol for performers, technicians, etc. Common sense is used by managers to prevent accidents.
- There is an informal understanding that bar staff and box office staff do not drink on duty.
- People in safety-critical areas who smell of alcohol will be sent home.
- People have occasionally been sent for counselling, paid for out of the company's health and safety budget.

Note
Managers would like to bring in with-cause testing and to seek agreement for this in staff contracts.

It is difficult to apply American findings in Europe, as there are differences in the way that health care costs are met. American evaluations of the cost–effectiveness of treatment are closely related to costs incurred by the company. These costs are different for companies in countries where health care is more the concern of the health services than the company, with costs spread across many taxpayers. Such cost estimates are not, therefore, included in company investment evaluations in some other countries. The perceived gains from running an alcohol policy may not, therefore, appear as attractive for companies in other countries. Recent legal changes in the United Kingdom, for instance, may serve to alter this situation, as from April 1994 employers must directly bear all sick pay costs (151); this could have the effect of making company health care policies more attractive.

Policies have also been shown to result in significant savings in factors other than health care costs. For example, Hiker (unpublished data, 1974) found that the introduction of an alcohol policy in the Illinois Bell Telephone Company produced a 46% reduction in sickness disability, an 81% decrease in on-duty accidents and a 63% decrease in off-duty accidents, resulting in an estimated annual saving for the company of US $1142 per person from wage replacement alone.

An important part of the evaluation of a policy is determining the effectiveness of the particular treatment used. This area of research is, however, substantial and will only be touched on here in the context of the effectiveness of inpatient compared to outpatient treatment and the relative costs involved.

Despite the body of evidence against the benefits of inpatient rehabilitation as compared to less intrusive treatments in the United States during the 1980s, a high proportion of employees were referred to inpatient care (152). It has been suggested that, although this reliance on inpatient care is not a cost-effective solution to the problem, it is one that was favoured for the following reasons (153).

1. Most medical insurance provides much fuller and sometimes exclusive coverage for hospital care.

2.   Sickness and accident plans cover employees' salaries while they are absent from work.

3.   An inpatient referral simplifies the Employee Assistance Pro-gramme (EAP) administrator's life. Managing an employee's entry into treatment is often a difficult, time-consuming and emotionally charged task. For a busy administrator, transferring that responsibility to an inpatient programme is clearly easier than personally having to orchestrate and monitor the client's successful integration into a non-residential alternative.

4.   The financial impact of these decisions may not be apparent to the administrator who makes them, as the costs of both the inpatient stay and the wage replacement can be buried elsewhere in the health benefit programme, under a jurisdiction that is generally quite separate from the EAP.

The success of "minimal" interventions, which cost significantly less than inpatient care, has been demonstrated in an evaluation of the Employee Counselling Service in Scotland *(154)*. This service accepts referrals from a wide range of employers in Scotland and devises counselling programmes to help those with alcohol-related problems. A year after receiving treatment, only 7.7% of clients had been dis-missed from their jobs as a result of their alcohol problem. (The study did not include a control group, however, which makes the results difficult to interpret accurately.) Other studies have demonstrated similar success. Anderson & Scott *(155)* assessed the effect of advice from their general practitioners on the drinking practices of men con-suming 350–1050 g of alcohol per week. In later comparison with a control group of men who had not been given any advice, those in the treatment group had significantly reduced their drinking (by an average of more than 65 g per week). Anderson & Scott conclude that the advice given was successful, and go on to recommend that general practitioners screen their patients for alcohol consumption and give advice to those who are found to be at risk due to heavy drinking. Wallace et al. *(156)* report the findings of a study involving 909 heavy drinkers (more than 350 g of alcohol per week). They found significant changes between a control and the intervention group, including a general reduction in alcohol use and fewer episodes of heavy drinking. The intervention programme used included brief advice from a physician on reducing or stopping alcohol use, a self-help booklet, weekly diaries to record alcohol use, and a written contract in the form of a prescription signed by the physician.

The effects of minimal interventions in reducing the amount of alcohol drunk by non-dependent drinkers has also been shown for a number of other countries. An intervention project sponsored by the World Health Organization *(157,158)* tested a brief intervention programme on 1661 non-dependent drinkers from ten countries with very different cultures and health care systems. The interventions assessed were *(a)* simple advice on abstinence and sensible drinking, *(b)* brief counselling involving a 15-minute session and a manual, and *(c)* extended counselling involving brief counselling and three or more monitoring visits. The results showed that the interventions had a significant effect in reducing both average alcohol consumption and intensity of drinking.

Problems with Evaluating the Success of a Policy

Evaluating the success of a particular policy, while being essential, is not a straightforward matter. The most common method is a simple before-and-after comparison based on observations of a number of key indicators (for example, accident rates, absenteeism and productivity). Although such a method provides some indications of success, the very complex nature of companies means that great care needs to be exercised when ascribing outcomes to a particular cause. It is likely that the effects of policies are often overestimated because the investigator tends to also be the administrator, who has a vested interest in presenting a positive image to senior managers. It is also the case that many reported evaluations appear in journals that are not peer reviewed, an essential process in maintaining academic rigour *(159,160)*.

There is also concern that researchers often do not look at workplace systems, and that they:

> do not investigate the workplace processes that motivate employees to change their behaviors and the actions of assistance workers that help employees to change their behaviors. Without understanding such things, professionals cannot interpret the findings of even the most elegantly designed outcome studies. ... Once researchers gain an

understanding of these processes ... they may evaluate the program outcomes more rigorously *(161)*.

In addition, Warner *(162,163)* points out that some of the costs of health promotion in the workplace have gone wholly unrecognized, namely pensions, later health care and disability payments for employees who remain alive due to the success of a programme.

There are also a number of methodological difficulties with many of the evaluations published to date. Richmond et al. *(83)* make the point that most do not include a control group and that follow-up periods are variable and/or too short to show long-term maintenance of behavioural change. There are also problems with the type of data needed to conduct an adequate assessment. Indicators of the effectiveness of a programme, such as changes in absenteeism, number of sick days, accidents, staff turnover, quality of job performance, number of disciplinary actions and estimates of work efficiency, are often not available or are measured in ways that are scientifically unacceptable. In addition, causal relationships between such measures and alcohol consumption may be hard to demonstrate. Absence, for example, may be taken to indicate levels of alcohol consumption, but may also reflect other factors such as commitment and job satisfaction. Furthermore, company records are designed to serve the needs of the organization and not those of researchers *(83)*.

The rate of penetration within the organization is used by some researchers to indicate the success of a programme. Penetration rate refers to the extent to which a programme reaches and affects all the workers in a company. This concept is derived from the public health model and contrasts with approaches that evaluate only employees who choose to participate. It is based on the assumption that there is a group "at risk" within the population and that the intervention can be regarded as successful if it reaches them. Success is therefore a function of the outreach of the programme within the organization *(159)*. This approach has a number of problems.

• It assumes that an estimate of the prevalence of the at-risk group is available. In the case of alcohol, however, this prevalence figure is difficult to obtain due to problems with self-reported data.

- It makes no attempt to evaluate the clinical effects of the treatment. There would be no advantage to high penetration if the treatment outcomes were poor.

The evaluations that have been discussed here indicate that the provision of treatment for employees with alcohol-related problems is cost-effective. In a review of alcohol treatment and health care costs, Holder & Cunningham *(164)* state that: "the cumulative evidence of studies based on employees and members of their families has revealed a decline in overall health care costs following alcoholism treatment".

In addition to the provision of treatment, the reduction of levels of drinking in non-dependent heavy drinking employees by the use of minimal intervention strategies also appears to be a cost-effective way of reducing alcohol problems. The possible economic benefits of using such procedures within companies are at the moment unknown, but could be significant.

Alcohol policies can encourage the identification of problem drinkers and bring a number of benefits to the company, including a reduction in the level of drinking at the workplace and also, where employees can be retained, savings in training costs associated with employing new staff. There are, however, costs associated with such action, particularly the cost of holding a post open while the employee seeks help, the costs associated with running a policy, and the cost of treatment that might fall to the employer. While such costs may be prohibitive, especially to the smaller employer, they may be seen as justifiable in relation to the benefits that can be achieved.

EDUCATION

Provision is often made, within a company's alcohol policy, for educating the workforce about drinking and the levels of alcohol consumed that may be injurious to their health, and about the possible consequences of working while intoxicated, and for publicizing the company's policy (an essential component of running a successful policy). The inclusion of education for all company employees enables a policy to address the wider issues surrounding alcohol use and the introduction of an "alcohol" as opposed to an "alcoholism" policy.

The inclusion of alcohol education as an integral part is now a feature of the policies of a number of large companies. Many companies invest significant amounts of money in publicity campaigns, involving the dissemination of the policy to all employees, frequent poster campaigns and even videos. Excerpts from two policies that include elements of education are provided below (see also a description of implementing policies in the British National Health Service (165)).

To prevent abuse of alcohol or drugs, the Strathclyde Passenger Transport Executive (PTE) aims to make employees aware that any consumption or taking of alcohol or drugs may adversely affect work performance. Employees will be given guidance in avoiding consumption of alcohol in quantities and at times which may lead to impairment during periods of work.

Over the years, Shell has provided training programmes and education to employees about the dangers of substance abuse. Training programmes will continue to be used to educate the employees and managers about substance abuse, how to recognise the warning signs, and what to do about them.

IS EDUCATION EFFECTIVE?

Cyster & McEwen (166) conducted a pre- and post-alcohol education evaluation involving 4000 Post Office employees who completed questionnaires. Responses indicated that, of the three different methods of presentation used, the most effective in increasing participants' knowledge about alcohol issues was an educational video; this was followed by participation in a quiz, with educational pamphlets being the least effective. Cyster & McEwan found that one of the problems with an employer initiating an alcohol education campaign was that it could be perceived as interference with employees' spare-time activities. To minimize this problem it is suggested that trade unions as well as management should be involved in the campaign, and that alcohol education should exist within the context of general health promotion.

In an attempt to assess the likely success of educational campaigns at the workplace, an investigation into some of the results from the more prevalent school-based health education research may be of use. DeHaes & Schuurman *(167)*, for example, demonstrated that a shock-horror approach to reducing alcohol and drug use was actually counterproductive, in that it led to an increase in the very behaviour it was designed to reduce. The choice of an appropriate education programme is therefore of crucial importance if it is to be successful. It is now generally accepted by educationalists that an approach combining facts and life skills may be the most effective way of educating young people about drugs and alcohol. It remains to be seen, however, which approaches are effective for educating adults. In addition to the form of the education message, other elements affect the success of an educational campaign; these include the perceived credibility of the sources of information and the educator, and also factors relating to the social and physical environment *(168,169)*.

5

Testing and Screening

This chapter reviews some recent developments regarding the testing of employees for alcohol. While it principally deals with issues related to alcohol, it also includes information about testing for other drugs. The reason for this is that many of the procedures being developed to test for the use of illegal drugs can also be used to test for alcohol. In addition to this, many of the ethical considerations that are important in testing for illegal drugs are also important for alcohol. Finally, alcohol use and drug use (both legal and illegal) are often included under one policy – a general drugs policy. In such cases procedures for the detection and control of their use will be similar.

Testing for alcohol and drugs originated in the United States Department of Defense during the 1960s as a response to drug use among military personnel returning from Viet Nam. Private companies then began to inquire about the legality of such testing, and some initiated procedures to screen employees and job applicants *(170)*. Since then, testing has become more prevalent internationally as a means of detecting instances of inappropriate drinking, with many companies now testing for alcohol use in cases where there is a "just cause" and as a follow-up to treatment. The excerpt from Shell Expro's drug and alcohol abuse policy below gives information as to the rules relating to with-cause testing and follow-up testing after treatment.

> With-cause [testing] – in safety sensitive areas. It [testing] will be carried out whenever workplace factors such as physical appearance, behaviour, other job-related circumstances give good faith reasons to question whether the employee may be impaired by drugs or alcohol

i.e. where he/she has the presence of illegal or illicit drugs or alcohol above the test cut-off levels in his/her system ...

Follow-up – when an employee returns to work following rehabilitation treatment for substance abuse. An initial test for drugs and alcohol use and abuse may be performed prior to an employee's return to work. Thereafter, periodic testing for both drugs and alcohol may be conducted as part of the company's efforts to assist the employee in avoiding a relapse.

In addition to with-cause and follow-up testing, random or unannounced testing is also beginning to be used. Such an indiscriminate method, though controversial, has a number of advantages in that it can potentially identify those drinkers who have previously been able to avoid detection (see Chapter 1). Random testing therefore aims to provide a deterrent to all instances of drinking.

OBJECTIVES

There are a number of ways in which testing can be carried out, and also a number of different parts of the workforce to which testing programmes can apply. The following section describes the objectives of five different types of programme.

Pre-employment screening may be used:

- to exclude users of certain substances from becoming part of the workforce or to stop users changing to certain jobs; or

- to deter the use of such substances among applicants.

With-cause testing may be used:

- to confirm or disconfirm the supervisor's or manager's suspicion that an employee has contravened the company's rules relating to alcohol; or

- to deter the use of prohibited substances among employees.

Routine testing, for employees in safety-sensitive positions, may be used:

- to prevent harm or loss to the public, the employer, fellow employees and the employees themselves; or

- to deter the use of prohibited substances.

Random testing may be used:

- to deter the use of prohibited substances among all employees; or

- to prevent and reduce harm or loss to the public, the employer, fellow employees and the employees themselves.

Follow-up testing may be used:

- to aid the effectiveness of treatment by deterring further use and identifying relapse; or

- to prevent or reduce harm or loss to the public, the employer, fellow employees and the employees themselves.

THE TRADE UNION RESPONSE

Although unions generally accept the need for measures to control the consumption of alcohol at the workplace, their principal concern is that any procedures are justified and implemented fairly. The following are some of the objections that have been raised about the introduction of testing programmes.

- Testing should be about assessing the competence of someone to perform a specific job rather than being introduced as a way of controlling employees' behaviour. This has proved an important point in Canada, where the unions agree with the Canadian Civil Liberties Association and the Canadian Human Rights Commission who state that, regardless of a positive test or a refusal to undergo such a test, the employer would have to demonstrate the employee's inability to perform the job.

- As testing can be used to harass employees, certain safeguards need to be included in the programme. There is a fear that drug testing may be used to purge "undesirable" employees from the workplace, or that it could be used to determine the employability and/or future productivity of employees *(171)*.

- The concept of "voluntary" submission to a test may be more apparent than real. In real life, a refusal to undergo a test may carry certain connotations, whether these are justified or not. The employee is therefore under some covert pressure to comply with requests to submit to a test.

- The introduction of testing may be more a result of political pressure than a desire to improve working conditions. Practices motivated by such factors may not always be in the best interests of the workforce.

- Testing can be viewed as an invasion of the individual's right to privacy, blood tests as intrusive, and direct observation of urination as degrading and a violation of personal rights (172).

Complaints that have arisen so far about testing, however, appear to be concerned more with policy implementation at local level, such as allegations of victimization by managers, than with the philosophy behind it (151). The stance taken by unions in the United Kingdom is illustrated by the Rail, Maritime and Transport Union (RMT), which represents staff at both London Underground and British Rail. While this union regrets the need for testing, it appreciates that it is prompted by legislation and is necessary in some circumstances. The RMT, however, does not advocate testing in all circumstances and states that random testing is "wasteful and ineffective and represents an unjustified infringement of employee rights, and as such should be opposed where possible" (151). Ideally, the RMT believes that testing should serve as a safety audit, and that the main long-term focus of alcohol and drug policies should be on education and awareness.

LEGAL ASPECTS

The United States

During the late 1980s the United States enacted important legislation that opened the door to the widespread introduction of screening programmes. In 1986 the President signed an executive order promoting the establishment of drug-free federal workplaces. An anti-drug abuse act was also passed, and guidelines on drug testing programmes for federal employees were introduced. As a result, random drug screening programmes have now been implemented by the US Department of Transportation to cover aviation, rail, mass transit, trucking and pipelines *(170)*.

MacDonald & Wells *(170)* make the point that the workplace is perhaps the best place for a screening programme. They state that:

> ... because 70% of all drug users are employed, the workplace may be the most strategic point in society from which to combat the scourge of drugs. Constitutional safeguards in many industrialized countries, such as rights to privacy and due process, can be bypassed through government regulation or agreements between employers and employees. Such measures can make drug screening in the workplace a very powerful detection tool for drug use in society.

While the by-passing of constitutional safeguards is a very contentious issue, testing at the workplace – if it can be achieved – would undoubtedly provide a powerful method for detecting levels of drug and alcohol use, not only in the work context but in society as a whole. American institutions are also attempting to introduce such procedures in collaboration with other countries. For example, the US Coast Guard hopes to achieve bilateral agreements with European countries and Canada in an attempt to introduce mandatory drug testing in all forms of transport and pipeline operation *(173)*. The stringent rules being applied in the United States will have a number of implications for other countries, particularly in multinational industries where American policies are being applied elsewhere.

The United Kingdom

Although there are no legal requirements for systematic testing in the United Kingdom (apart from certain instances relating to with-cause tests) a number of companies are beginning to introduce it as a result of the Transport and Works Act of 1992, which requires employers to show "all due diligence" to avoid any alcohol-related accidents. The Act also gives a number of powers to the police with regard to testing employees who they have reason to believe are under the influence of alcohol (see Chapter 2).

The introduction of random testing in the United States has met with a number of difficulties, including those relating to the employee's constitutional right to privacy which, in effect, means that employees cannot be dismissed for refusing to undergo a random test. No similar constitutional right exists in the United Kingdom, which means that dismissal for refusal to take a test cannot be challenged in the common law courts so long as the employers have abided by the conditions outlined below.

First, employers have a legal duty not to "breach the implied term of mutual trust and confidence". When applied to drug testing, this means that employers are legally bound to keep the information about drug tests strictly confidential while informing the employee of the results, even though there may be no explicit contractual relationship to do so (Howard, G., unpublished data, 1992). If, however, the testing is carried out before employment, the potential employer has no legal obligation to disclose the results of the test.

Second, employers are obliged to include the conditions of testing in the contract of employment in order to permit them to test staff. The following is an example of such an inclusion (Howard, G. unpublished data, 1992).

> At any time whilst on duty, or on Company premises, or for the purposes of taking up employment, you will provide, upon request from a duly authorized person from the Company's Occupational Health Service, a specimen of breath and/or urine for the purpose of screening for alcohol and prohibited drugs. Any failure to comply will be a disciplinary offence which may render you liable to dismissal.
>
> This agreement constitutes your consent to the conclusions of any screening referred to above being passed to the Board of Directors or a senior member of management by any authorized person.

If employers want to introduce testing, it can be put into the contract of employment for new staff. This does not, however, apply to existing staff; they may be offered a new contract that includes the testing requirement, but are under no legal obligation to accept it. This can cause resentment between new and existing staff owing to differences in their conditions of employment. Also, without a contractual agreement to testing, employers have no legal right to force any staff to consent to a test. If an employer flouts this rule, then it is possible for the employee to resign and claim "constructive dismissal" at an industrial tribunal hearing. In any such case related to testing, the tribunal would take account of all issues relevant to the case, which could include:

- whether there had been consultation prior to the introduction of the testing requirement;

- whether the introduction and procedures surrounding testing had been discussed with the trade unions;

- whether a competent person had explained to the employee the reasons for testing and the nature of the tests;

- whether confidentiality had been assured;

- whether correct testing procedures had been adhered to; and

- whether the individual had been counselled as to the consequences of his or her refusal, given time to consider it, and warned formally about continued refusal.

If an employee is tested and a positive result is found, retesting is usually carried out on a second sample taken at the same time as the first and stored in a secure place. If a test result is disputed in court, the finding will depend on "current protocols, procedures and controls, and whether these had been adopted". The courts will also look at whether the analysis of the sample and the conclusions reached were "conclusions that any reasonably competent professional would have reached" (Howard, G., unpublished data, 1992).

PROCEDURAL AND SECURITY STANDARDS

The procedural and security standards for testing both at the workplace and in the laboratory are important in any industrial tribunal case involving alcohol or drug testing. Some of the current recommendations for testing procedures are as follows (174–176).

- It is important that samples of blood and urine are taken by two qualified medical personnel (such as a doctor and a nurse), securely labelled, appropriately and securely stored, and taken to the testing laboratory immediately after the collection procedure is completed.

- The analyses of urine or blood samples, for alcohol or drugs, should be conducted only by personnel with appropriate and documented qualifications.

- All personnel must follow laboratory procedures and security standards.

- The laboratory should be secure at all times, and access should be limited to authorized personnel only.

- The laboratory should establish security measures to guarantee that specimens are properly received, documented, processed and stored. Documentation of "chain of custody" procedures should include receipt of specimen, results during storage, and final disposal of specimen.

- The laboratory must comply with any government licence requirements, be inspected routinely, keep appropriate documentation and procedural manuals, and use properly certified equipment.

- Urine specimens should be inspected immediately on arrival at the laboratory to ensure that they have not been tampered with during delivery.

- Specimens should be stored in a secure refrigeration unit if they are not tested within 7 days of arrival at the laboratory. The storage temperature should not exceed 6 °C; long-term storage must be at −20 °C to ensure that drug/alcohol-positive urine specimens do not deteriorate and will be available for any retesting during administrative or disciplinary proceedings. The laboratory may be required to maintain any specimen under legal challenge for an indefinite period.

- At present, initial testing (which eliminates the alcohol-negative samples) usually consists of an immunoassay technique. This should be followed up by confirmatory tests on drug/alcohol-positive samples, which should employ a different technique and chemical principles from the initial test. At present, gas chromatography/mass spectrometry is the recommended confirmation method.

The use of such stringent procedures means that the laboratory costs of analysis are high and can be a substantial burden for a company running a testing programme. Costs associated with such procedures are considered a necessary expense, as without them results would not have any validity in an industrial tribunal.

METHODS AND INTERPRETATIONS

Of particular importance to any testing programme are the procedures and methods used to obtain test samples. These are crucial, as the legality of test results and any action taken as a result of the test depend on the stringency of the testing procedures. Alcohol policies that include testing must therefore include detailed procedures for the collection and analysis of samples.

There are a number of methods for assessing the amount of alcohol that a person has drunk. These include tests on the blood, urine and breath. Each test has its own advantages and disadvantages.

Blood

Advantages

- Blood tests provide an accurate measure. Correlation with the degree of impairment is usually stronger for blood alcohol levels than for urine alcohol or breath alcohol levels.

Disadvantages

- The collection of a blood sample is an invasive procedure that can be distressing.

- Blood is available only in relatively small quantities. This has ramifications for conducting multiple tests on particular samples – tests that may be required as part of the standard testing and legal procedures.

- The absolute quantity of alcohol in the blood depends not only on the amount consumed but also on the length of time that has elapsed since it was consumed. This limits the usefulness of blood tests for determining the degree of intoxication when blood is collected some time after the event. Although previous alcohol levels may be estimated (the amount of alcohol eliminated from the body is a linear function approximately equivalent to one unit per hour) the calculation is not precise as the rate of elimination varies with age, sex and physical condition *(177)*.

- The enzyme responsible for oxidizing alcohol is also present in red blood cells and will slowly metabolize the alcohol in the sample. This can, however, be prevented by adding sodium fluoride *(178)*.

- The results take time to process, making the technique unsuitable for on-site monitoring.

Urine

Advantages

- Urine requires a less invasive technique for its collection than blood.

- Urine is available in larger quantities than blood, making additional tests and repeated analyses easier to conduct.

Disadvantages

- Urine testing is less accurate than blood testing.

- Like blood testing, it can be difficult to estimate accurately the level of consumption when samples are taken some time later.

- Excretion of alcohol in urine and its concentrations can be affected unpredictably by dilution and the pH (acidity) of the urine.

- Large amounts of alcohol can be produced in the urine samples of diabetic patients (during storage). Diabetics must therefore be identified so that their samples can be processed immediately.

- Urine testing is the method whereby employees can most easily cheat the system. Samples can be substituted, and it is interesting to note that testing has already been associated with the creation of a black market in "clean" urine *(179)*. Some people adulterate their urine with substances such as bleach. Drinking large amounts of water prior to urinating also poses problems for the laboratories.

- The results take time to process.

Breath

Advantages

- Breath testing is non-invasive.

- The costs are low.

- Testing produces immediate results.

Disadvantages

- The accepted 2100:1 alveolar breath:blood conversion ratio used for breathalysers *(180)* has been shown to consistently under-estimate actual blood alcohol concentrations *(181)*.

- The accuracy of the test can be influenced by instrumental and biological factors *(182,183)*.

- Errors can be caused by residual alcohol in the mouth. Although this effect should disappear after 20 minutes, artificially high values lasting for as long as 45 minutes have been reported *(184)*.

Blood testing would therefore appear to give the most accurate indication of the alcohol level in the body. It might not be considered suitable for routinely testing employees as it is expensive and intrusive. The method used will depend on the severity of the situation and also on the type of test being conducted (with-cause or random). One solution to this problem is to employ the use of a non-intrusive method to obtain an initial sample, and use the result from this as a basis on which to justify the use of a more accurate test. For example, an initial test might be conducted with a breathalyser and any positive results followed up with a blood test.

THE CREDIBILITY OF TESTS

Testing for alcohol and drugs, when conducted properly, involves extremely accurate measurements and strict adherence to procedures. The accuracy of the measurements, the "scientific" manner in which everything is done and the often high cost give a strong impression that the results are "correct" and "credible". There is evidence, however, that although the presence of a substance can be detected very accurately, there is a danger of some false results that can have serious consequences for employees and employers. A false-positive result can have devastating and unfair consequences for an employee. Apart from the financial hardship incurred by losing a job, there is social stigma surrounding alcohol-related problems or drug use. False-positive tests are also of concern to employers as they can result in the loss of good employees, problems of morale and potential law suits.

Alcohol and drug tests will not always be positive for samples that contain the substance (false-negative) and may be positive for those that do not contain the substance (false-positive) *(185)*. As the consequences of a false-positive test are so serious for an employee, the false accusation rate of tests should be carefully monitored. The false accusation rate is the probability that the specimen contains no alcohol or drugs but gives a positive test result. To calculate this rate, at least three pieces of data are required: the substance-use rate for the target group of workers, the false-positive rate of the laboratory conducting the testing, and the true-positive rate of the testing laboratory.

> Although empirical studies of drug-testing laboratory proficiency always report conventional accuracy indicators such as the false positive and true positive rates, neither positive predictive values nor false accusation rates have ever been reported in these proficiency studies *(186)*.

It is essential to know the false accusation rate of a drug testing process before deciding whether the test result provides credible evidence of drug use. However, this information is not commonly provided. Furthermore, "the role of the false accusation rate as an indicator of the credibility of evidence has not been explored or operationalized in the industrial relations literature" *(186)*.

The current situation regarding the credibility of testing can be summed up as follows.

> The proportion of positive drugs tests that are false, that is, the false accusation rate, can be high even when tests themselves are judged extremely accurate by conventional laboratory measures. In such cases, positive drugs tests do not provide credible evidence of drug use. Our estimates of drug use, false positive rates, and true positive rates, all of

which are based on recently published empirical evidence, indicate that under common circumstances, drug testing results have high false accusation rates and hence low credibility (186).

It is suggested by Barnum & Gleason (186) that the credibility of test results can be assured by setting an "acceptable" false accusation rate. The false accusation rate drops with repeated confirmations of the test results; if levels are unacceptably high, repeated confirmations will ensure that the rate falls to an acceptable level. Until laboratories produce the false accusation rate, it is not possible to have confidence in the credibility of the results currently produced.

OUTCOMES ASSOCIATED WITH TESTING PROGRAMMES

The hypothetical effects of testing programmes include reduced alcohol or drug use, fewer accidents at the workplace, lower absenteeism, increased productivity and fewer disciplinary actions. Given the investment of time and money, which is a necessary part of instigating a testing programme, it would be useful to know the actual impact and effectiveness of the measures. Unfortunately, however, current knowledge about overall gains from testing is inconclusive. This is due to the sparseness of research in this area and the fact that the research that does exist is often found wanting in terms of scientific rigour (170). Calculation of the economic effects of testing can only be guesswork at the present time since, as with the calculation of costs associated with alcohol use in general, there is no agreement on the appropriate method for estimating costs or even on which factors should be included in the estimate.

There is, however, some published research that purports to demonstrate the positive impacts of testing programmes. For example, research at General Motors has indicated that, following the onset of a drug screening programme, absenteeism fell by 40%, disciplinary actions decreased by 50% and the number of accidents fell by 50% (187). Likewise, an electrical utility company reported a 25% drop in absenteeism following the introduction of a testing programme (188). The United States Navy found that the percentage of drug-positive tests dropped to 5% (from a level of 48% when testing was first introduced) following the implementation of a regular programme of

61

testing *(189)*. Testing can therefore play a significant role in changing workplace behaviour. It should be noted, however, that the methodology of many studies on the impact of testing programmes has been criticized. Often, reductions in accident rates, increases in productivity and decreases in substance use are attributed to testing without accounting for the effects of other developments such as education and treatment. Also, many of the studies fail to describe the type of testing programme implemented or the consequences of a positive test, both of which are of crucial importance to the outcome of the testing programme *(190–192)*.

Researchers have also hypothesized the potential negative outcomes of random testing, which is the most controversial form of testing used *(193)*. These outcomes can include increased feelings of insecurity, oppression and anxiety in employees which, it is argued, may lead to reduced productivity *(194)*. The criticisms generally levelled against random testing are that it violates individual privacy and that it has the potential to be misused, in that it is possible for disliked employees to be victimized. In addition, it is an inefficient and costly method of screening, as most of the tests carried out are negative *(193)*. If random testing is used fairly and the procedures are communicated adequately to the employees, however, it has the advantage that it does not single out employees as potential drug or alcohol users *(195)*. Random testing is also believed to be one of the most effective deterrents against drug use *(196)*.

There are a number of other negative effects of alcohol and drug testing programmes. For instance, post-accident testing may lead to minor accidents not being reported for fear of the consequences of an alcohol-positive test *(191,194)*. Another problem is that a positive test may provide some justification for apportioning blame for an accident, although it may not in itself rule out other causal factors. In this case, alcohol use may be wrongly identified as a causal factor. The use of probable-cause testing can result in certain employees being identified as possible alcohol users on the basis of behavioural signs that may not be related to alcohol use at all. It is possible that certain symptoms may be misdiagnosed and lead to the singling out and labelling of individuals who are not misusing alcohol or drugs *(195)*. The usefulness of pre-employment testing is difficult to assess, as prospective employees may stop taking drugs while they are applying but resume once they are in the post. In addition, there is no method of assessing whether those rejected would have actually posed problems for the company. As employers do not have to provide the results of pre-employment testing to prospective employees, or give them a reason for their rejection, this type of testing is perhaps the one that is most open to abuse. Unfortunately, it raises the fewest trade union objections, as unions do not have to represent the interests of non-members *(187,196)*.

Other research has suggested that screening methods in general can reduce morale *(179,197–200)*, undermine employee–management relations and promote legal action against companies *(199)*. The use of a testing programme can even have consequences for the type of applicants a company receives. Crant & Bateman *(201)* discovered that companies that screen may be less likely to receive job applications from non-users as well as users. The reason for this seems to be related to the way in which potential applicants view the company. Applicants tended to have a more positive attitude towards companies that did not have a testing programme, and viewed these companies as more trusting and less invasive of the privacy of their employees. It is, however, unclear at present whether such a covert selection process works to the company's benefit or not.

In conclusion it appears that, although testing may reduce general levels of drug use among employees, the introduction of a programme has many other consequences. While the reduction of alcohol and drug use and their associated problems are a desired outcome for many employers, drug testing may also lower staff morale and disrupt employer–employee relationships. It is, at the present time, unclear if testing programmes do provide significant economic gains and under which conditions these gains may be maximized. Before an answer to this question can be attempted, rigorous scientific research is needed to clarify the whole range of costs and benefits associated with all methods of testing.

PREVALENCE OF TESTING IN INDUSTRY

The United States

The prevalence of screening programmes in the United States varies as a function of the type of work performed by the companies. A 1988 survey of medium-size and large corporations indicated that manufacturing firms and companies in the utility and transportation sectors were most likely to have testing programmes; and that companies in banking, insurance and other financial services were least likely to have such programmes. Also, companies that had a programme of screening tended to be relatively large, with a substantial workforce and operating from several sites *(202)*.

In general, the larger the company the more likely it is to have a testing programme. In 1986, 25% of the largest 500 companies had testing programmes *(203)* compared to only 3.2% of companies overall, a figure that had increased to 4.4% by 1990 *(197)*. More recent evidence indicates that in 1992, 85% of American corporations used some form of testing *(204)*. This survey may not be representative of American business, however, as it was directed at corporations and only included those companies that responded to the survey. As it is mostly the larger companies that have policies, the proportion of *employees* covered by a testing programme is likely to be significantly higher than the figures quoted for the proportion of *companies* that have policies. It would be useful to estimate the proportion of the population covered by testing programmes, but unfortunately this information does not appear to be available. The extent of the use of testing in the United States can, however, be gauged to some extent by estimates that some 20% of American workers were tested in 1992 *(186,204,205)*.

The most popular type of screening (as measured by the number of companies who use it) is pre-employment screening, with random testing being the least popular method. Of the companies with testing programmes, 92% used pre-employment testing, 77% used probable-cause testing, 12% used periodic screening and only 8% tested randomly *(206)*.

Europe

Compared to the United States, there is little research on the prevalence of testing in Europe, possibly because testing there is a more recent development.

It is believed that the recent introduction of testing in the United Kingdom came about principally as a result of the 1992 Transport and Works Act, although this Act does not explicitly state that companies must operate testing programmes. The Transport and Works Act calls on employers to use "all due diligence" in preventing the use and abuse of alcohol and drugs in the workplace. It is likely that many companies will equate this with the setting up of a testing programme.

As a response to the Transport and Works Act, the British Transport Police gave details of the first 14 months of a testing operation between 7 December 1992 and 28 February 1994 (see Table 3). These tests were undertaken by London Underground and British Rail.

Table 3. Details of testing conducted by the British Transport Police

	London Underground	British Rail
Tests administered	57	181
Positive tests	12	33
Tests refused	8	7
Prosecutions in progress	16	30
Convictions to 28 February 1994	1	15

Source: Incomes Data Services *(151)*.

A study of 111 European companies estimated that 30 (27%) used an employee testing programme *(207)*. In this study it was also estimated that 18% of companies implemented pre-employment testing; of these, 72% tested for alcohol and the remainder tested only for illegal and/or prescribed drugs. Details of the programmes used or under consideration in the companies are outlined in Table 4.

Table 4. Testing policies in use or under consideration in 30 European companies in 1993

When testing conducted	No. currently testing for:		No. considering testing for:	
	alcohol	drugs	alcohol	drugs
Randomly for all employees	4	1	3	3
Randomly for employees in safety-sensitive jobs	7	6	3	4
During periodic medical examination for certain staff	11	8	1	3
Following accidents or incidents at work as required	13	10	2	2
Following concern or suspicion by management	13	7	1	2
As part of a treatment programme	11	9	2	3

Source: Smith (207).

Table 5. Reasons given by 30 companies for introducing a testing programme

Reason	No. of companies
General concern about reducing accidents	19
General concern about reducing the prevalence of alcohol- and/or drug-related problems	15
Specific legal or legislative requirements	6
Following a specific alcohol- or drug-related incident at the workplace	5
Following testing practices in other organizations	4
Following the policy adopted by a parent or sister organization	2
A commitment to reducing illegal drug use in society	2

Source: Smith (207).

Asked why they had implemented testing, companies revealed that they were motivated by a wish to reduce alcohol- and drug-related problems, or because of legislation. The companies that did not test did not do so because they were concerned about the impact of testing on the legal and civil liberties of their employees, and the potential negative consequences on employee–employer relationships that could result (see Tables 5 and 6).

Table 6. Reasons given by 28 companies for not introducing a testing programme

Reason	No. of companies
The position of testing *vis-à-vis* legal and civil liberties is unclear	19
Testing may adversely affect employee–employer relations	16
Alcohol and other drug problems could be detected more efficiently using existing resources and available procedures	9
Testing is inconsistent with the organization's ethical beliefs	9
Will reassess the situation when other organizations have testing policies in place	4

Source: Smith *(207)*.

6

Coverage of Alcohol Policies

It is estimated that only a small proportion of companies have formal written policies, although most appear to operate at least an informal agreement *(208)*. This chapter reviews some of the published estimates of the proportion of companies that operate a policy covering alcohol-related problems. While such studies are not ideal for providing estimates of the proportion of the working population covered by such a policy, their inclusion in the present review is justified as they at least provide some useful information.

METHODOLOGICAL PROBLEMS

Accurate estimates of the overall number of companies operating alcohol policies, and the overall number of employees covered by an alcohol policy, are difficult to provide as numbers are usually calculated using survey data, which has a number of serious limitations. For example, in a survey of company policies on alcohol problems, it is those companies that are already aware of the issues that are most likely to respond to a questionnaire. The questionnaires returned are likely, therefore, to include a higher proportion of companies active in the field and ultimately exaggerate estimates of the number of companies nationally that have policies. Response rates are therefore an important indication of the representativeness of a particular study.

The method of recruitment used is likely to have a major effect on the results of a survey. This is demonstrated by comparing the results of two studies, one using subscribers to the Alcohol

Awareness magazine *Grapevine (208)* and another using a sample more representative of the country as a whole *(100)*. Differences in the two studies are to be expected, as subscribers to *Grapevine* are likely to be already aware of alcohol issues. This is reflected in the fact that the first survey found 76% of companies to have one or more policies covering alcohol at work, while the second reported only 32%. Comparisons between surveys are also made difficult because the criteria used for what constitutes a policy often differ, as do the locations in which the studies were carried out *(209,210)* and the size of the companies included.

There is also quite a serious problem when interpreting the results of the studies in that it is unclear what exactly was being measured. For instance, it is not always clear what constitutes "having an alcohol policy". Is it the mere possession of a policy that is being measured or is its implementation considered as well? This has important implications, as companies recorded as having a policy may not even adhere to it. Other companies may actually operate a policy, but if it is implemented under casual understandings or under a different title (such as a sickness or health policy) it may not be recorded as an alcohol policy. These studies, therefore, can often only show the proportion of companies that have something written down about alcohol misuse. The studies do, however, give some idea of prevalence.

THE PROPORTION OF COMPANIES THAT IMPLEMENT POLICIES

There are a number of studies that provide estimates of the proportion of companies in the United Kingdom operating an alcohol policy of one type or another. Of these, Brittan et al. *(100)* provide what is perhaps one of the most comprehensive pictures of current practices in British industry, and give information on the type of approach that is most commonly adopted. In their study, three groups of companies could be identified: those who made no special provisions for alcohol, those who recognized the problem but had not implemented any measures, and those who had carefully worked out strategies to deal with issues regarding alcohol use at work. They estimated the proportion of companies to have embarked on positive action to be about

32%. This figure is slightly higher than that found by O'Brien & Dufficy *(141)* who estimated the proportion to be no more than 20%. MEL Research Ltd (unpublished data, 1994) in a study conducted on a representative sample of companies in inner-city Birmingham, estimated that only 23% have an alcohol policy, a relatively low figure compared to the 40% found in a study by the Industrial Relations Service *(208,211,212)* and to the 33%, estimated by Howie & Carter *(213)* for major employers in Fife, Scotland. Many of these figures are, however, likely to overestimate the overall proportion of companies in the United Kingdom that operate policies. A more realistic figure is that provided by Powell (unpublished data, 1990) who reviewed a number of studies and concluded that fewer than 20% of firms in the United Kingdom had formal workplace policies designed to reduce employment costs associated with alcohol consumption.

British industry appears to be behind that of the United States in the adoption of alcohol policies *(214)*, the proportion of American companies with formal workplace policies being estimated at about 60%. The proportion of British companies with formal policies is likely to increase, however, as those that are aware of the problems but have not yet introduced policies bring them into force (24% of companies studied by Brittan et al. *(100)* fell into this category). A number of factors will tend to encourage companies to adopt policies: the publication of figures showing the proportion of the workforce having alcohol problems at work *(215)*; estimates of the financial costs that inappropriate drinking may incur *(99,104)*; the effect of recent health campaigns *(216,217)*; the publication of the Government's health policy *(5)*; and laws relating to alcohol use at work.

The Importance of Company Size

The relationship between the size of the company and whether it operates a policy is shown clearly in a study by the Industrial Relations Service *(208,211,212)*. Only 16% of British companies employing 101–200 people had a policy, compared with 70% of those employing more than 10 000 people. While comparison of these results is difficult, as sample sizes are likely to be very different (there are comparatively very few companies with 10 000 employees or more), the relationship between company size and the existence of a policy would appear to be obvious. This effect has also been demonstrated in the United States, where 70% of the largest 500 companies *(218)* have developed alcohol policies on the counselling, treatment and support of employees, compared with only 51% of medium-sized companies.

IMPROVING COVERAGE

One of the major goals of agencies active in the alcohol field is to increase the proportion of companies that operate alcohol policies and thereby increase the proportion of the workforce covered by them. Substantial increases in the overall proportion of the workforce covered by alcohol policies will depend on increases in the number of smaller companies that introduce them.

One of the major reasons identified for small companies not operating alcohol policies is that they often do not believe that they have a problem with alcohol. This may indicate that many smaller companies do not actually have a problem, but may also indicate a lack of knowledge about the effects that alcohol use at work can have *(219,220)*. Few employers in smaller companies appear willing to recognize that they may have a problem *(221)*, a result echoed in the findings of a recent survey of small to medium-size companies (10–200 employees) conducted in Liverpool *(222)*. In this survey, 65% of respondents reported that alcohol had never caused problems during the working day. Assuming that 10% of the adult population are drinking at levels that may be injurious to health (a figure often quoted to justify alcohol policies) a number of companies employing between 10 and 50 people will not have any problems associated with alcohol use. Chadwick & Pendleton *(222)* suggest, however, that companies who carry out a systematic look at their workplaces might indeed find evidence of the effect that alcohol is having.

In addition to the problem of recognizing instances of alcohol-related harm, small companies may not introduce formal policies owing to the resources and organization that this entails. A large proportion of the policies currently in use were initiated by occupational health departments, personnel managers or health and safety managers *(208)*, which many smaller organizations do not employ. The lack of resources can be overcome to some extent by the

71

use of outside agencies, which can provide, for example, relevant literature, materials on health promotion, advice on constructing a policy, and counselling for employees with alcohol problems. This may prove to be a viable option for a number of companies, as it can substantially cut the cost of addressing alcohol-related problems. Most outside agencies either do not charge or charge only a small amount for copies of their materials (223).

If more of the smaller companies are to consider introducing alcohol policies, further consideration needs to be given to the factors that will motivate them to do so, such as the potential costs of alcohol use (particularly by a key employee), the likely effect that alcohol has in their particular circumstances, and the ways in which problems might be tackled. The creation of an alcohol policy in a small company will also often require the use of resources outside the company. Small companies may also be more likely to introduce policies for alcohol consumption as part of a policy covering a whole range of health issues. Policies addressing the issue of alcohol use may, for example, be more attractive when introduced as part of a broader policy that also deals with smoking and drug use (27,166).

Germany

The use of external organizations to support and encourage companies in tackling the problems related to alcohol appears to be common practice in Germany. The German Addiction Centre (*Deutsche Hauptstelle gegen die Suchtgefahren*, DHS) is a national centre for information, research and library services, disseminating information and statistics throughout Germany (224–226). The German National Centre for Health Education (*Bundeszentrale für Gesundheitliche Aufklärung*, BZgA) also produces information about alcohol and has developed a wide-ranging package about issues surrounding alcohol in the workplace (135). It states, for instance, that "at least 5% of all employees are alcoholic, and a further 10% are seriously at risk from alcohol abuse" and that these employees are 16 times more likely to be absent, and to be involved in occupational accidents 3.5 times as often. It also explains German legislation relevant to alcohol at the workplace; for example, industrial accidents caused by employees even with very low blood alcohol levels are not covered by occupational accident insurance. It encourages companies to consider primary prevention measures, such as removing the availability of alcohol, education on alcohol, stress reduction and improvements in working hours. It also advises about the early recognition of alcohol-related problems and recommends early treatment. It encourages these measures to be formalized in a company alcohol policy, and gives examples of policies.

Within Germany there are also a number of separate regional organizations that give information and support. Over the last five years the *Landesstelle Berlin gegen die Suchtgefahren* (LBS) has:

> developed a regional service centre for Berlin, with a team of management trainers and consultants. It is aimed at companies and public organizations that are interested in addiction prevention and want to do something for their employees in this respect. During the process of initiation, implementation and establishment of these programmes, we consult them, sometimes over several years. Some companies are now ready to allow some first steps of evaluation to take place *(227)*.

LBS also participates in a cooperative network of organizations called DIALOG. This network is a forum for sharing information and advice.

German companies have access to an established information magazine called *Partner* (published every two months and similar to *Grapevine* published by the Health Education Authority in England) that aims to support companies dealing with alcohol-related problems.

Handwerker-Fonds (a union for craftspeople) specifically provides information for companies of 150 workers or fewer. This information includes the cost of alcohol problems, the effects of working conditions on addiction, how to identify problem drinkers, how the company can be helped internally and externally, legal information, special help for craftspeople, details of alcohol-related events and alcohol literature, and advice to managers on alcohol policies.

The United Kingdom

In the United Kingdom, organizations such as the Health Education Authority, the Alcohol Education and Research Council, Alcohol

Concern, the many regional councils on alcohol, and employee counselling services currently offer advice, literature, support and often employee counselling to companies setting up and running alcohol policies. Self-help groups such as Alcoholics Anonymous also counsel employees with alcohol-related problems without cost to the company. The use of such organizations would appear to be one way of making alcohol policies more attractive to small companies.

It is likely that the number of companies operating policies will increase in the future. The success of these policies will ultimately depend on the expertise and support provided by a number of outside agencies. If alcohol, smoking and more general health policies can be implemented in more companies it is likely that the benefits will spread to some extent to society as a whole. The task now appears to be to convince management that the operation of an appropriate policy could be to their and their employees' benefit.

7

Discussion

THE ECONOMICS OF ALCOHOL

There has been a substantial amount of research conducted in the area of alcohol use and its possible effect on industry. This research has often attempted to estimate a monetary value for the effects of alcohol consumption on industry as well as on economies as a whole. Although the overall "gains" that may be attributed to the alcohol industry (due to employment, trade and investment, for example) are an important part of the overall equation, it is the costs associated with alcohol that have attracted the most attention.

These costs have been calculated for a number of countries and are often estimated to form a substantial proportion of a country's gross national product. In the United Kingdom, for instance, the estimate most commonly quoted is in the region of £2 billion for 1987. This estimate includes a number of contributors to cost, such as sick leave, unemployment, premature death, costs incurred by the National Health Service, and alcohol-related criminal activities. It does not, however, include a number of the less easily quantifiable costs such as loss of productivity, accidents, staff turnover, disruptions to working relationships, and losses brought about by a poor company image. The non-inclusion of these factors has led some researchers to assert that the figures provided so far are underestimates, with the true costs being significantly higher. This belief may be challenged, however, on the grounds that the Human Capital – Cost of Illness (HC–COI) economic model often used to assess costs has limited validity, and also that the positive consequences of alcohol consumption are not taken into consideration.

A number of researchers have made use of the HC–COI model to estimate the costs associated with alcohol use. This model estimates costs on the basis of the potential worth of employees, a concept that may have limited validity when applied to countries where there is a degree of unemployment. Calculating costs by such a method produces a figure that is often far higher than would be obtained by estimating the direct costs associated with, for example, staff turnover, sickness payments and disruption to production. The estimates obtained for factors such as unemployment and premature death due to alcohol are the *potential* costs and not the *actual* costs (i.e. the money that may be saved) as is often assumed. In addition to the problems of applying this model, the benefits that may be attributed to alcohol use are usually not included in estimates of overall cost.

Almost all figures and statistics relating to the problem of quantifying costs are subject to the reservation that they are only estimates and approximate values of phenomena that at present cannot be recorded with scientific precision. DiNardo *(228)*, in a review of the costs of alcohol and drug use in the United States, concludes that the estimates of overall cost are of limited value, a criticism that can also be applied to studies conducted in the United Kingdom.

If the accuracy of estimates is to be improved, a number of issues need to be addressed, including the quality of data, the effects of alcohol on behaviour and health, and the interaction between alcohol use and other factors. At present, many of the data available have been collected to fulfil certain company needs rather than to answer specific research questions. As a result of this, many of the data are not suited to research purposes. For example, information about sick leave in the United Kingdom is most readily available in the form of employees' self-certified reasons for absence. The "reasons" identified by employees for their absences, however, bear little or no relationship to the actual causes, at least when these are due to excessive alcohol use. The data available on absence are therefore of little use for assessing the relationship between alcohol consumption and absenteeism. In addition to the protective effects that moderate consumption of alcohol can have on health, other beneficial effects may also affect the estimates of cost. In particular, estimates should be given for the value of alcohol when it is used as a reinforcer, and also estimates for the possible beneficial social effects it can have.

The effects of the interaction between alcohol and other types of behaviour (particularly smoking and stress) also need to be accounted for, as these have a number of implications for costs and are at present poorly understood.

A fundamental issue when estimating costs, and one that is often ignored, is the effect that researchers' expectations or beliefs can have in determining which factors are to be included in the cost estimate. Such decisions are crucial, as they ultimately determine to a large degree the size of the estimate. For example, the expectation that all alcohol use has negative consequences and leads to a cost will inevitably highlight the potential costs and encourage them to be included in the estimate. The same encouragement does not apply to the potential benefits. DiNardo *(228)* makes the point that researchers are more likely to accept imprecise negative results than they are to accept positive estimates, and that this tendency to ignore the imprecision of negative estimates or the occasional "anomalous" positive estimates fundamentally undermines any claims made by the authors.

In addition to the difficulties of assessing costs associated with alcohol use are the difficulties in assessing the impact that reducing or eliminating alcohol consumption would have. As alcohol is only one of a number of substances that an individual can choose to consume, a certain amount of substitution may occur if there is a reduction in the amount taken of a particular substance. People may well turn to alternatives. Increases in the use of marijuana, for example, can lead to reductions in the use of other drugs (Modal, K.E., unpublished data, 1993); similarly, a reduction in the use of heroin often leads to an increase in the use of alcohol *(229,230)*. A decrease in the use of alcohol can lead to increases in the use of prescribed drugs *(231)* and tobacco *(232)*. Reducing or eliminating the use of alcohol is therefore unlikely to lead to a "saving" equivalent to the estimated cost associated with alcohol use. Unfortunately, the assumption often implicit in estimates of the cost of alcohol use is that this is the amount of money that would be saved if its use were eliminated; this does not appear to be the case.

Even if these problems could be solved, it is questionable if much would be gained by establishing better estimates of overall cost. Solving these mainly practical problems might indeed improve the overall accuracy of the calculation of monetary costs, but would do little to counter some of the other problems in putting an economic value on alcohol use. These other problems include estimating the cost of such things as personal freedom, enjoyment and improvement in the quality of life that alcohol can bring. These factors need to be taken into account if the calculations of "cost" are to have any real validity at all.

Not all estimates of cost, however, are subject to the same criticisms. The use of a cost–benefit calculation can be helpful, at least when evaluating the effects of certain policy alternatives. A cost–benefit analysis allows the analyst to generate reliable estimates without a complete description of the many and subtle links between alcohol consumption and its outcome measures. Although such a system cannot provide an indication of overall cost, it can indicate the relative effectiveness of a number of alternative policies. The use of a cost–benefit analysis framework may be of particular use to companies (more use than the assessment of overall costs) as it enables answers to questions such as "Will productivity be enhanced by introducing alcohol policy X?".

Although current estimates are so unreliable, they are very much in demand as they provide a means of gauging overall alcohol-related costs, which are useful in directing public opinion and government policy. A number of commentators have stated that it may, however, be a mistake to use such estimates as a guide to making priorities on spending, as they do not rest on a firm economic base. Guyot *(233)* goes further and states that the economic argument has no economic reality, but it is perceived as being of use in that it allows politicians to pinpoint "the problem" and justify their measures.

INDUSTRY'S RESPONSE TO ALCOHOL

Even though there are significant problems with estimating the effects of alcohol consumption in overall monetary terms, it has been demonstrated to many people's satisfaction that the use of alcohol, at least in some situations, can create significant problems for industry. In response to this, it appears that industry is now beginning to recognize and address alcohol-related problems. The motivation to do so has come mainly from the publication of research that has identified some of the possible associated costs, and also from legislation.

Industry's key response to alcohol-related problems has been to introduce alcohol policies into the workplace. Alcohol policies are able to aid in the detection, disciplining and rehabilitation of employees with alcohol-related problems, as well as in educating the workforce about the likely effects of alcohol consumption and about safer drinking practices. The benefits that may be achieved through the introduction of an alcohol policy include a safer, healthier, better motivated workforce as well as a number of economic gains, including those that can be achieved through the rehabilitation of employees who may otherwise have been unproductive or dismissed.

The way in which alcohol dependency is viewed has serious consequences for the establishment of procedures for dealing with employees who have, or can demonstrate, alcohol-related problems. Although the status of alcohol dependency as an illness is disputed, employers are encouraged to treat it as such. Industrial tribunals have more or less adopted this framework, and often require companies to make the same kinds of provision for those suffering from an alcohol-related problem as are made for those who are suffering from any other "illness". Such a requirement can sometimes lead to the seemingly absurd situation whereby an employer dismisses a productive, non-problem drinking employee while retaining a less productive problem-drinking employee *for the same offence*. This apparent double standard can create a certain amount of resentment, and has even led some employees to claim that they have an alcohol-related problem when this is not in fact the case.

Alcohol policies are designed to deal with problems once they have been identified, but they can also be used to identify potential problems by encouraging employees to express any concerns they may have about alcohol before it becomes a matter of discipline. Such a strategy typically involves the offer of treatment while the employee's job is safeguarded. This encourages employees to get help for any drinking problems and, at the same time, enables the employer to reduce the overall level of drinking at the workplace. An alcohol policy, therefore, has potential advantages for both employees and employers. It can provide procedures for dealing with alcohol-related problems once they have arisen and, through the pro-vision of treatment to employees on a voluntary basis, can even reduce the number of disciplinary cases related to alcohol use.

An important function of any alcohol policy, and one that is unfortunately often neglected, is to identify those aspects of the work-place and/or aspects of work that encourage drinking. Certain work-ing practices and working environments exert a powerful influence on levels of drinking, and can work against the establishment of appro-priate drinking norms. Employees may respond to the more immedi-ate and powerful understanding of "what is acceptable" than to the company's rules about drinking at work. To be as successful as pos-sible, policies need to address the effects that such understandings and working practices have on behaviour, and change them if possible. The implementation of an appropriate alcohol policy provides one way in which an employer can do this. One method of changing overall behaviour at the workplace is to introduce a more general alcohol education programme. Such programmes can change the behaviour of employees by educating them about the company alcohol policy, about the effects of drinking, and about the limits within which it is safe to drink. Although it is unclear at present how effective education campaigns actually are in altering drinking behaviour, they have been shown to be successful in disseminating information and their inclusion in alcohol policies is therefore justified.

In recent years, one of the major and most controversial devel-opments in attempting to reduce the incidence of alcohol problems at work has been the introduction of testing. The major forms of testing used so far include random, with-cause, post-treatment, periodic and pre-employment. The introduction of such tests has come about, at least partly, as a result of legislation that makes employers potentially liable, jointly with the offending employee, for incidents involving alcohol. Although the legislation may not explicitly require the intro-duction of testing programmes, it encourages employers to introduce them by requiring that "all due diligence" is shown in avoiding alcohol- or drug-related accidents. In addition, giving the police the power to test and arrest without warrant those suspected of having alcohol in their body gives a clear signal as to what "due diligence" might actually mean.

One of the major considerations for the success of alcohol policies, and one of paramount importance to industry, is whether they are cost–effective. It is difficult at present to know with any certainty whether the introduction of an alcohol policy will result in any gains for a company. Research in the United States has indicated that the provision of treatment for "alcoholics" can result in substantial savings for a company. However, this research cannot easily be applied to other countries, as there are major differences in health care systems and in the liabilities of the companies involved. It is also likely that estimates of the overall cost of treatment in the United States may be artificially high, owing to a number of reasons that are often not related to the effectiveness of treatment. Recent findings indicate that a relatively cheap, minimal intervention can be just as effective as inpatient care. The provision of minimal interventions will make treatments cheaper and, as a result, make comprehensive alcohol policies more attractive and open to a greater number of employees. Before any definite answers can be given as to the cost–effectiveness of alcohol policies, a considerable amount of research needs to be conducted in the area, not only into the effectiveness of different forms of treatment but also into which employees would be most likely to benefit.

It is estimated that only a small proportion of companies have an alcohol policy (although the actual percentage of the working population covered by such policies is likely to be higher). This percentage is, however, likely to increase substantially as the effects of legal developments, health-related campaigns (particularly with regard to smoking) and the publication of figures showing the possible extent of the problem begin to take effect. Given that it is the smaller companies that are least likely to operate a policy, future efforts should concentrate on identifying the specific needs of smaller companies and on the development of resources that will enable companies to introduce a policy.

A number of agencies encourage the widespread adoption of alcohol policies and believe that this will benefit the country as a whole. For example, the Confederation of British Industry *(14)* advocates the introduction of alcohol policies and reminds employers that:

... terminating the employment of a drug-taking employee could result in a complaint of unfair dismissal. ... In any event, termination of employment is a short-term solution to the problem. The only result is that the employee will carry the problem to another employer – and you in your turn will be hiring the result of similar antisocial attitudes by other companies.

Such an attitude may be absent in a number of companies that may still dismiss employees with alcohol-related problems and rehire, perhaps taking the precaution of using pre-employment testing to minimize the possibility of employing someone with a similar problem. Such a short-term solution may work for individual companies but is unlikely to improve matters on a national level, as no effort has been made to address the individual's difficulties. Costs have merely been transferred from one company to another, or on to the state.

In conclusion, it appears that alcohol policies, either as part of specific policies on alcohol or as part of more general drug and health policies, will become more common within industry and will apply to greater numbers of employees in the future. The widespread introduction of policies will inevitably result in certain restrictions on employees' behaviour. This may be justified, however, as the potential improvements for employers and employees may outweigh any of the disadvantages associated with restricting personal freedom. Some of the likely consequences of the more widespread use of policies are a reduction in accident rates, a reduction in alcohol-related mortality, increased productivity and the establishment of a better informed workforce. The latter is particularly important, as this will enable all employees to make more informed choices about their own drinking behaviour. This in turn could result in significant changes, not only in patterns of workplace drinking but also in patterns of drinking in society as a whole.

References

1. *National health survey of alcohol consumption, Australia (1989–1990)*. Canberra, Australian Bureau of Statistics, 1991.

2. WILLIAMS, G.D. & DEBAKEY, S.F. Changes in levels of alcohol consumption: United States, 1983 to 1988. *British journal of addiction,* **87**(4): 643–648 (1992).

3. WILLIAMS, G.D. ET AL. *Apparent per capita alcohol consumption: national, state, and regional trends, 1977–1989.* Washington, DC, US Government Printing Office, 1991 (NIAAA Surveillance Report No. 20).

4. *Alcoholic beverages and European society.* London, Amsterdam Group, 1993.

5. *The health of the nation: a strategy for health in England.* London, H.M. Stationery Office, 1992.

6. MOSER, J. *Alcohol problems, policies and programmes in Europe.* Copenhagen, WHO Regional Office for Europe, 1992 (document EUR/ICP/ADA 011).

7. STAUDENMEIER, W.J., JR. *Alcohol in the workplace: a study of social policy in a changing America.* St Louis, MO, Washington University, 1985.

8. WARNER, J. Good help is hard to find: a few comments about alcohol and work in preindustrial England. *Addiction research,* **2**(3): 259–269 (1995).

9. LEVIN, H.G. Industrialization, economic development, and worker drinking: historical and sociological observations. *In: Legislative approaches to prevention of alcohol-related problems.* Washington, DC, National Academy Press, 1982.

10. BAGGOTT, R. *Alcohol, politics and social policy.* Aldershot, Avebury, 1990.

11. MCGREGOR, D. *The human side of enterprise.* New York, McGraw-Hill, 1960.

12. MCGREGOR, D. *The professional manager.* New York, McGraw-Hill, 1967.

13. MASLOW, A.H. *Motivation and personality.* New York, Harper and Row, 1954.

14. *Working for your health: practical steps to improve your business.* London, Confederation of British Industry, 1993.

15. JELLINEK, E.M. What shall we do about alcoholism? *Vital speeches,* **13**: 252–253 (1947).

16. MAXWELL, M.A. Early identification of problem drinkers in industry. *Quarterly journal of studies on alcohol,* **21**: 655–678 (1960).

17. MAXWELL, M.A. Alcoholic employees: behavior changes and occupational alcoholism. *Alcoholism,* **8**: 174–180 (1972).

18. TRICE, H.M. The job behavior of problem drinkers. *In:* Pittman, D. & Snyder, C.R., ed. *Society, culture and drinking patterns,* New York, Wiley, 1962, pp. 493–510.

19. PELL, S. & D'ALONZO, C.A. Sickness absenteeism of alcoholics. *Journal of occupational medicine,* **12**: 198–210 (1970).

20. MAXWELL, M.A. A study on absenteeism, accidents, and sickness payment in problem drinkers in one industry. *Quarterly journal of studies on alcohol,* **20**: 302–312 (1959).

21. THORPE, J.J. & PERRY, J.T. Problem drinking: a follow-up study. *Archives of industrial health,* **19**: 24–29 (1959).

22. MORAWSKI, J. ET AL. Economic costs of alcohol abuse, with special emphasis on productivity. *In: The negative social consequences of alcohol use.* Oslo, Norwegian Ministry of Health and Social Affairs and Vienna, United Nations, 1990, pp. 95–128.

23. BROSS, M.H. ET AL. Chemical dependence: analysis of work absenteeism and associated medical illnesses. *Journal of occupational medicine,* **34**: 16–19 (1992).

24. TRICE, H.M. & ROMAN, P.M. *Spirits and demons at work.* New York, Cornell University, 1978.

25. MARTIN, J.K. ET AL. Extent and impact of alcohol and drug use problems in the workplace: a review of the empirical evidence. *In:* MacDonald, S. & Roman, P., ed. *Research advances in alcohol and drug problems. Vol. 11. Drug testing in the workplace.* New York and London, Plenum Press, 1994.

26. NORMAND, J. ET AL. *Under the influence? Drugs and the American workforce.* Washington, DC, National Academy Press, 1994.

27. JOEMAN, L.M. *Alcohol consumption and sickness absence: an analysis of 1984 General Household Survey data.* London, Department of Employment, 1992 (Research Series No. 4).

28. HUTCHESON, G.D. ET AL. *Alcohol in the workplace: costs and responses.* London, Department of Employment (in press).

29. JONES, G.A. Alcohol abuse and traumatic brain injury. *Alcohol health and research world,* **13**(2): 105–109 (1989).

30. WINTEMUTE, G.J. ET AL. Alcohol and drowning: an analysis of contributing factors and a discussion of criteria for case selection. *Accidents, analysis and prevention,* **22**(3): 291–296 (1990).

31. HURST, P.M. Epidemiological aspects of alcohol in driver crashes and citations. *Journal of safety research,* **5**(3): 130–148 (1973).

32. NATIONAL HIGHWAY TRAFFIC SAFETY ADMINISTRATION. *Alcohol and highway safety 1984: a review of the state of knowledge.* Washington, DC, US Department of Transportation, 1985 (Technical Report No. DOT-HS-806-569).

33. PERRINE, M.W. Epidemiologic perspectives on drunk driving. *In: Surgeon General's workshop on drunk driving: background papers.* Washington, DC, US Department of Health and Human Services, 1989, pp. 35–76.

34. SUMMALA, H. & MIKKOLA, T. Fatal accidents among car and truck drivers: effect of fatigue, age and alcohol consumption. *Human factors,* **36**(2): 315–326 (1994).

35. ZADOR, P.L. Alcohol-related relative risk of fatal driver injuries in relation to driver and age and sex. *Journal of studies on alcohol,* **52**(4): 302–310 (1991).

36. OLKKONEN, S. & HONKANEN, R. The role of alcohol in non-fatal bicycle injuries. *Accidents, analysis and prevention,* **22**(1): 89–96 (1990).

37. TRANSPORTATION RESEARCH BOARD. *Zero alcohol and other options: limits for truck and bus drivers.* Washington, DC, National Research Council, 1987 (Special Report 216).

38. TRANSPORTATION RESEARCH BOARD. *Alcohol and other drugs in transportation: research needs for the next decade.* Washington, DC, National Research Council, 1993.

39. CHERPITEL, C.J. Breath analysis and self-reports as measures of alcohol-related emergency room admissions. *Journal of studies on alcohol,* **50**(2): 155–161 (1989).

40. CHERPITEL, C.J. Prediction of alcohol-related casualties: a comparison of two emergency room populations. *Drug and alcohol dependency,* **24**: 195–203 (1989).

41. HOLT, S. ET AL. Alcohol and the emergency service patient. *British medical journal,* **281**: 638–640 (1980).

42. WECHSLER, H. ET AL. Social characteristics and blood alcohol level: Measurements of subgroup differences. *Quarterly journal of studies on alcohol,* **33**(1): 132–147 (1972).

43. YATES, D.W. ET AL. Alcohol consumption of patients attending two accident and emergency room departments in North-West England. *Journal of the Royal Society of Medicine,* **80**(8): 486–489 (1987).

44. YATES, D.W. The detection of problem drinkers in the accident and emergency department. *British journal of addiction,* **82**(2): 163–167 (1987).

45. GOODMAN, R.A. ET AL. Alcohol and fatal injuries in Oklahoma. *Journal of studies on alcohol,* **52**(2): 156–161 (1991).

46. CHERPITEL, C.J. Alcohol and injuries: a review of international emergency room studies. *Addiction,* **88**: 923–937 (1993).

47. CHERPITEL, C.J. ET AL. Alcohol and casualty in the emergency room. A U.S.–Italy comparison of weekdays and weekend evenings. *Addiction research,* **1**(3): 223–238 (1993).

48. OUVRARD, C. Approche du coût économique et social de l'alcoolisation en milieu du travail. *In: Alcool et économie.* Paris, CNCDA, 1986.

49. RASZEJA, S. [Causes and mechanisms of trauma at work. Forensic–medical and epidemiological analysis.] *Archiwum medycyny scadowej i kryminalistyki,* **26**: 157–164 (1976).

50. LEWIS, R.J. & COOPER, S.P. Alcohol, other drugs, and fatal work-related injuries. *Journal of occupational medicine,* **31**: 23–28 (1989).

51. ALLEYNE, B.C. ET AL. Alcohol and other drug use in occupational fatalities. *Journal of occupational medicine,* **33**: 496–500 (1991).

52. HEALTH AND SAFETY EXECUTIVE. *The problem drinker at work.* London, H.M. Stationery Office, 1981.

53. LEDERMAN, D. & METZ, B. Les accidents du travail et l'alcool. *Population,* **15**: 301–316 (1960).

54. POPHAM, R.E. ET AL. Heavy alcohol consumption and physical health problems: a review of the epidemiological evidence. *In: Research advances in alcohol and drug problems, Vol. III.* New York, Plenum Press, 1984, pp. 149–182.

55. ECKARDT, M.J. Health hazards associated with alcohol consumption. *Journal of the American Medical Association,* **246**(6): 648–666 (1981).

56. ANDA, R.F. ET AL. Alcohol and fatal injuries among U.S. adults. *Journal of the American Medical Association,* **260**(17): 2529–2532 (1988).

57. EMERY, M. Alcohol and safety in industry. *Journal of social and occupational medicine,* **36**: 18–23 (1986).

58. MORAWSKI, J. & MOSKALEWICZ, J. Casualties in Poland: focus on alcohol. *In: Drinking and casualties.* London, Routledge, 1989, pp. 245–259.

59. MORAWSKI, J. *Uwarunkowania nietrzezwosci i alkoholizmu pracowników duzego zakladu przemyslowego* [Sobriety and alcoholism among workers in large industrial enterprises]. Warsaw, Institute of Psychiatry and Neurology (Research Report No. 21/Alc/76).

60. STRÖMBERG, C. ET AL. Acute effects of maprotiline, doxepin and zimeldine with alcohol in healthy volunteers. *Archives of international pharmacodynamics,* **291**: 217–228 (1988).

61. PETERSON, J.B. ET AL. Acute alcohol intoxication and cognitive functioning. *Journal of studies on alcohol,* **51**: 114–122 (1990).

62. ERWIN, C.W. ET AL. Effects of buspirone and diazepam, alone, and in combination with alcohol, on skilled performance and evoked potentials. *Journal of clinical psychopharmacology,* **6**: 199–209 (1986).

63. COLLINS, W.E. Performance effects of alcohol intoxication and hangover at ground level and at simulated altitude. *Aviation, space, and environmental medicine,* **51**: 327–335 (1980).

64. FOLTIN, R.W. ET AL. Behavioural effects of ethanol and marijuana, alone and in combination with cocaine in humans. *Drug and alcohol dependence,* **32**: 93–106 (1993).

65. BLUM, T.C. ET AL. Alcohol consumption and work performance. *Journal of studies on alcohol,* **54**: 61–70 (1992).

66. CRITCHLOW, B. Blaming the booze: the attribution of responsibility for drunken behaviour. *Personality and social psychological bulletin,* **9**(3): 451–473 (1983).

67. CRITCHLOW, B. The powers of John Barleycorn: beliefs about the effects of alcohol on social behaviour. *American journal of psychology,* **41**: 751–764 (1986).

68. LEIGH, B.C. Venus gets in my thinking: drinking and female sexuality in the age of AIDS. *Journal of substance abuse,* **2**(2): 199–213 (1990).

69. REINARMAN, C. & LEIGH, B.C. Culture, cognition and disinhibition: notes on sexuality and alcohol in the age of AIDS. *Contemporary drug problems,* **14**(3): 435–460 (1987).

70. GUSTAFSON, R. Alcohol and aggression: a test of an indirect measure of aggression. *Psychological report,* **60**: 1241–1242 (1987).

71. GUSTAFSON, R. Male physical aggression as a function of alcohol, frustration, and subjective mood. *International journal of addiction,* **26**(3): 255–266 (1991).

72. PERNANEN, K. *Alcohol in human violence.* New York, Guilford Press, 1991.

73. WELTE, J.W. & ABEL, E.L. Homocide: drinking by the victim. *Journal of studies on alcohol,* **50**(3): 197–201 (1989).

74. DAVIES, J.B. Drinking and alcohol problems in five industries. *In:* Hore, B. & Plant, M., ed. *Alcohol problems in employment.* London, Croom-Helm, 1981.

75. *United Kingdom alcohol statistics.* Glasgow, Scottish Council on Alcohol, 1994.

76. GODDARD, E. *Drinking and attitudes to licensing in Scotland.* London, H.M. Stationery Office, 1986.

77. GODDARD, E. & IKIN, C. *Drinking in England and Wales in 1987.* London, H.M. Stationery Office, 1988.

78. UNITED NATIONS. *Yearbook of industrial statistics, Vol. II.* New York, United Nations, 1965–1980.

79. WALSH, B.M. Production of and international trade in alcoholic drinks: possible public health implications. *In:* Grant, M., ed. *Alcohol policies.* Copenhagen, WHO Regional Office for Europe, 1985 (WHO Regional Publications, European Series, No. 18).

80. WALSH, B.M. & GRANT, M. *Public health implications of alcohol production and trade.* Geneva, World Health Organization, 1985.

81. GRANT, M. Establishing priorities for action. *In:* Grant, M., ed. *Alcohol policies.* Copenhagen, WHO Regional Office for Europe, 1985 (WHO Regional Publications, European Series, No. 18).

82. COLLINS, D.J. & LAPSLEY, H.M. *Estimating the economic costs of drug abuse in Australia.* Canberra, Department of Community Services and Health, 1991 (National Campaign against Drug Abuse, Monograph No. 15).

83. RICHMOND, R. ET AL. *National campaign against drug abuse: workplace policies and programs for tobacco, alcohol and other drugs in Australia.* Canberra, Australian Government Publishing Service, 1992 (Monograph Series No. 24).

84. KASURINEN, V. Alkoholin käyttöön liityvät haittakustannukset vuonna *[Costs associated with the harmful effects of alcohol use over the year].* Alkoholpolitiikka, **45**(5): 187–194 (1980).

85. KIESELBACH, K. Milliardenschaden durch Griff zur Flasche. *Die Welt,* 14 April 1993.

86. *Drug and alcohol testing in the workplace.* Geneva, International Labour Office, 1994.

87. CHETWYND, J. & RAYNER, T. Economic costs to New Zealand of lost production due to alcohol abuse. *New Zealand medical journal,* **98**(785): 694–697 (1985).

88. HANSEN, A. Niektóre spoleczno-ekonomiczne skutki nietrzezwosci zawodowej w gospodarce narodowej – dzis i jutro *[Some socioeconomic effects of occupational sobriety in the national economy].* In: *Skutki alkoholizmu w w zakladach pracy oraz spol eczno-prawne srodki przeciwdzialania. Konferencja naukowa* [Effects of alcoholism in enterprises and socio-legal ways of prevention. Scientific Conference]. Warsaw, IPISS, 1973.

89. HOLTERMAN, S & BURCHELL, A. *The costs of alcohol misuse.* London, H.M. Stationery Office, 1981 (Government Economic Service Working Paper No. 37).

90. MAYNARD, A. ET AL. Data note-9. Measuring the social cost of addictive substances. *British journal of addiction,* **82**: 701–706 (1987).

91. JACKSON, P. The cost of alcohol abuse. *Brewing review,* **19**: 1–2 (1988).

92. MAYNARD, A. The costs of addiction and the costs of control. *In:* Maynard, A. & Chester, R., ed. *Controlling legal addictions.* London, Macmillan, 1989.

93. BERRY, E.R. & BOLAND, J.P. *The economic cost of alcohol abuse.* New York, Free Press, 1977.

94. RICE, D.P. ET AL. *The economic costs of alcohol and drug abuse and mental illness: 1985.* San Francisco, US Department of Health and Human Services, University of California, 1990.

95. HARWOOD, H.J. ET AL. *Social and economic costs of alcohol abuse and alcoholism.* Research Triangle Park, NC, Research Triangle Institute, 1985.

96. BURKE, T.R. The economic impact of alcohol abuse and alcoholism. *Public wealth reports,* **103**(6): 564–568 (1988).

97. DUFFY, J.C. The epidemiology of risk assessment. *In:* Duffy, J.C., ed. *Alcohol and illness: the epidemiological viewpoint.* Edinburgh, Edinburgh University Press, 1992, pp. 1–18.

98. ANOKHINA, I. & IVANETS, N. The problems and logistics of alcohol research in different settings: the example of the USSR. *In:* Plant, M. et al., ed. *Alcohol & drugs: research & policy.* Edinburgh, Edinburgh University Press, 1990, pp. 46–55.

99. GODFREY, C. & MAYNARD, A. *A health strategy for alcohol: setting targets and choosing policies.* York, Centre for Health Economics, University of York, 1992 (YARTIC Occasional Paper No. 1).

100. BRITTAN, J. ET AL. *Alcohol in the workplace: a feasibility study. A report to the Department of Employment.* Universities of Hull and York, 1990.

101. ADELSTEIN, A. & WHITE, G. Alcoholism and mortality. *Population trends,* **6**: 7–13 (1976).

102. BARRISON, I.G. ET AL. Detecting excessive drinking among admissions to a general hospital. *Health trends,* **14**: 80–83 (1982).

103. LOCKHART, S.P. ET AL. Alcohol consumption as a cause of emergency general medical admissions. *Journal of the Royal Society of Medicine,* **79**(3): 132–136 (1986).

104. GODFREY, C. & HARDMAN, G. *Updating the social cost of alcohol misuse.* York, University of York, 1990.

105. BACKHOUSE, M. ET AL. *Problem drinkers and the statutory services. Report to the DHSS.* Universities of Hull and York, 1986.

106. ETTORE, E. A follow-up study of alcoholism treatment units: exploring consolidation and change. *British journal of addiction,* **83**(1): 57–65 (1988).

107. STOCKWELL, T. & CLEMENT, S. *Community alcohol teams.* London, Department of Health, 1989.

108. SERVICE DES STATISTIQUES DES ÉTUDES ET DES SYSTÈMES D'INFORMATION. *Morbidité alcoolique dans les hôpitaux publics et en médecine de ville.* Paris, Ministère des affaires sociales et de la solidarité nationale, 1978.

109. *Quelques statistiques économiques, sanitaires et financières.* Paris, Comité national de défense contre l'alcoolisme, 1980.

110. KRISTENSEN, H. *Studies on alcohol-related disabilities in a medical intervention programme in middle-aged males.* Malmö, University of Lund, 1982.

111. MUSTER, E. *Zahlen und Fakten zu Alkohol- und Drogenproblemen 1988.* Lausanne, Swiss Institute for the Prevention of Alcoholism, 1988.

112. UMBRICHT-SCHNEITER, A. ET AL. Alcohol abuse: comparison of two methods for assessing its prevalence and associated morbidity in hospitalized patients. *American journal of medicine,* **91**(2): 110–118 (1991).

113. CACES, M.F. ET AL. *Trends in alcohol-related morbidity among short-stay community hospital discharges, United States: 1979–1989.* Washington, DC, Government Printing Office, 1991 (NIAAA Surveillance Report No. 21).

114. ABEL, E.L. & SOKOL, R.J. Incidence of fetal alcohol syndrome and economic impact of FAS-related abnormalities. *Drug and alcohol dependence,* **19**: 51–70 (1987).

115. ABEL, E.L. & SOKOL, R.J. A revised conservative estimate of the incidence of FAS and its economic impact. *Alcoholism: clinical and experimental research,* **15**(3): 514–524 (1991).

116. CICERO, T.J. Effects of parental exposure to alcohol and other drugs. *Alcohol health and research world,* **18**(1): 37–41 (1994).

117. JACOBSON, J.L. & JACOBSON, S.W. Prenatal alcohol exposure and neurobehavioral development: where is the threshold? *Alcohol health and research world,* **18**(1): 30–36 (1994).

118. JONES, K.L. & SMITH, D.W. Recognition of the fetal alcohol syndrome in early infancy. *Lancet,* **2**: 999–1001 (1973).

119. RICE, D.P. The economic cost of alcohol abuse and alcohol dependence: 1990. *Alcohol health and research world,* **17**(1): 10–11 (1993).

120. LEIGH, B.C. Relationship of sex-related alcohol expectancies to alcohol consumption and sexual behaviour. *British journal of addiction,* **85**(7): 919–928 (1990).

121. LEIGH, B.C. Relationship of substance use during sex to high-risk sexual behaviour. *Journal of sex research,* **27**(2): 199–213 (1990).

122. ROOM, R. & COLLINS, G., ED. *Alcohol and disinhibition: nature and meaning of the link.* Washington, DC, US Department of Health and Human Services, 1983 (Research Monograph 12).

123. MORGAN THOMAS, R. Alcohol, drugs and sexual behaviour. *In:* Plant, M. et al., ed. *Alcohol and drugs: the Scottish experience.* Edinburgh, Edinburgh University Press, 1992, pp. 34–40.

124. BLOSS, G. The economic costs of FAS. *Alcohol health and research world,* **18**(1): 53–54 (1994).

125. MCDONNELL, R. & MAYNARD, A. The costs of alcohol misuse. *British journal of addiction,* **80**: 27–35 (1985).

126. MAJEWSKA, A. Przyczynek do badan nad wplywem alkoholizmu na absenccéw pracy *[Contribution to research on the effect of alcoholism on absenteeism at work]. Walka z alkoholizmem,* No. 10, pp. 17–21 (1960).

127. HEALTH AND SAFETY EXECUTIVE. *The costs of accidents at work.* London, H.M. Stationery Office, 1993. (Health and Safety Series Booklet HS(G)96).

128. OFFICE OF POPULATION CENSUSES AND SURVEYS. *The 1990/91 Labour Force Survey.* London, H.M. Stationery Office, 1992.

129. DAVIES, N.V. & TEASDALE, P. *The costs to the British economy of work accidents and work-related ill health.* Sudbury, Health and Safety Executive Books, 1994.

130. US GENERAL ACCOUNTING OFFICE. *Controller General's report to subcommittee on alcoholism and narcotics.* Washington, DC, Government Printing Office, 1970.

131. KREITMAN, N. Alcohol consumption and the preventive paradox. *British journal of addiction,* **81**: 353–363 (1986).

132. SCHOLLAERT, P. Job-based risks and labour turnover among alcoholic workers. *In:* Schramm, C., ed. *Alcoholism and its treatment in industry.* Baltimore, Johns Hopkins Press, 1977, pp. 177–185.

133. COOPER, C.L. & SADRI, G. The impact of stress counselling at work. *Journal of social behavior and personality,* **6**(7): 411–423 (1991).

134. CYSTER, R. ET AL. *Alcohol policies: a guide to action at work.* London, The Industrial Society, 1987.

135. *Alkoholprobleme in der Arbeitswelt. Ein Seminarkonzept betrieblichen Alkoholprävention.* Kassel, Bundeszentrale für Gesundheitliche Aufklärung, 1988.

136. FILLMORE, K.M. Research as a handmaiden of policy: an appraisal of estimates of alcoholism and its cost in the workplace. *Journal of public health policy,* **4**: 40–64 (1984).

137. AMES, G.M. ET AL. Obstacles to effective alcohol policy in the workplace: a case study. *British journal of addiction,* **87**: 1055–1067 (1992).

138. TRICE, H.M. Work-related risk factors associated with alcohol abuse. *Alcohol health and research world,* **16**(2): 106–111 (1992).

139. PLANT, M.A. *Drugs in perspective.* London, Hodder & Stoughton, 1987.

140. *Bargaining report.* London, Labour Research Department, 1986.

141. O'BRIEN, O. & DUFFICY, H. The nature of the problem. *In:* Dickenson, F., ed. *Drink and drugs at work: the consuming problem.* Institute of Personnel Management, 1988, pp. 12–21.

142. HINGSON, R. ET AL. Job characteristics and drinking places in the Boston metropolitan area. *Journal of studies on alcohol,* **42**(9): 725–738 (1981).

143. ROMAN, P.M. & TRICE, H.M. The development of deviant drinking behaviour: occupational risk factors. *Archives of environmental health,* **20**: 424–435 (1970).

144. MANNELLO, T.A. ET AL. *Problem drinking among railroad workers: extent, impact, and solutions.* Washington, DC, University Research Corporation, 1979.

145. AMES, G.M. & JANES, C. A cultural approach to conceptualizing alcohol and the workplace. *Alcohol health and research world,* **16**(2): 112–119 (1992).

146. DAVIES, J.B. Reported alcohol consumption, and attitudes of managerial and non-managerial employees, in a study of five Clydebank industries. *British journal of alcohol and alcoholism,* **13**(4): 160–169 (1979).

147. HASIN, D. ET AL. Multiple alcohol-related problems in the United States: on the rise? *Journal of studies on alcohol,* **51**(6): 485–493 (1990).

148. *Alcohol policy guidelines for health authorities.* London, Health Education Authority, 1992.

149. BLOSE, J.O. & HOLDER, H.D. The utilization of medical care by treated alcoholics. Longitudinal patterns by age, gender, and type of care. *Journal of substance abuse treatment,* **3**: 13–27 (1991).

150. HOLDER, H.D. & BLOSE, J.O. The reduction of health care costs associated with alcoholism treatment: a 14-year longitudinal study. *Journal of studies on alcohol,* **53**(4): 293–302 (1992).

151. *Alcohol and drug policies.* London, Incomes Data Services, 1994.

152. EDWARDS, G. ET AL. Alcoholism: a controlled trial of "treatment" and "advice". *Journal of studies on alcohol,* **38**(5): 1004–1031 (1977).

153. WALSH, D.C. ET AL. Treating the employed alcoholic: which interventions work? *Alcohol health and research world,* **16**(2): 140–148 (1992).

154. MCALLISTER, P.O. An evaluation of counselling for employer-referred problem drinkers. *Health bulletin,* **51**(5): 285–294 (1993).

155. ANDERSON, P. & SCOTT, E. The effect of general practitioners' advice to heavy drinking men. *British journal of addiction,* **87**: 891–900 (1992).

156. WALLACE, P. ET AL. Randomized controlled trial of general practitioner intervention in patients with excessive alcohol consumption. *British medical journal,* **297**: 663–668 (1988).

157. BABOR, T.F. ET AL. Verbal report methods in clinical research on alcoholism: response bias and its minimization. *Journal of studies on alcohol,* **48**(5): 410–424 (1987).

158. SAUNDERS, J. & AASLAND, O. *WHO collaborative project on the identification and treatment of persons with harmful alcohol consumption. Report on Phase One: development of a*

screening instrument. Geneva, World Health Organization, 1987.

159. KURTZ, N.R. ET AL. Measuring the success of occupational alcoholism programs. *Journal of studies on alcohol,* **45**(1): 33–45 (1984).

160. LUTHANS, F. & WALDERSEE, R. What do we really know about EAPs? *Human resources management,* **28**(3): 385–401 (1989).

161. SONNENSTUHL, W.J. The job-treatment balance in Employee Assistance Programs. *Alcohol health and research world,* **16**(2): 129–133 (1992).

162. WARNER, K.E. Selling health promotion to corporate America: uses and abuses of the economic argument. *Health education quarterly,* **14**(1): 39–55 (1987).

163. WARNER, K.E. Wellness at the worksite. *Health affairs,* Summer 1990, pp. 63–79.

164. HOLDER, H.D. & CUNNINGHAM, D.W. Alcoholism treatment of employees and family members. *Alcohol health and research world,* **16**(2): 149–153 (1992).

165. HAYES, G. Implementing alcohol polices in the NHS. *In:* Doogan, K. & Means, R., ed. *Alcohol and the workplace.* Bristol, School for Advanced Urban Studies, 1990, pp. 120–130.

166. CYSTER, R. & MCEWEN, J. Alcohol education in the workplace. *Health education journal,* **46**(4): 156–161 (1987).

167. DEHAES, W. & SCHUURMAN, J. Results of an evaluation study of three drug education models. *International journal of health education,* **18**: 1–16 (1975).

168. HENDERSON, M.M. ET AL. *Evaluation of health and HIV/AIDS education.* Paisley, Argyll and Clyde Health Board, 1993.

169. ROCHE, A.M. Drug and alcohol medical education: evaluation of a national programme. *British journal of addiction,* **87**: 1041–1048 (1992).

170. MACDONALD, S. & WELLS, S. The impact and effectiveness of drug testing programs in the workplace. *In:* MacDonald, S. & Roman, P., ed. *Research advances in alcohol and drug problems. Vol. II: Drug testing in the workplace.* New York and London, Plenum Press, 1994, pp. 121–142.

171. ALVI, S. Union perspectives on workplace drug testing. *In:* Macdonald, S. & Roman, P., ed. *Research advances in alcohol*

and drug problems. Vol. II. Drug testing in the workplace. New York & London, Plenum Press, 1994, pp. 305–317.

172. MACDONALD, S. ET AL. *Issues related to drug screening in the workplace.* London, Ontario, Addiction Research Foundation, 1992.

173. GLASS, J. *USCG puts drug testing on hold.* London, Lloyds List, 1992.

174. KWONG, T. Critical issues in urinalysis of abused substances. Report of the substance-abuse testing committee. *Clinical chemistry,* **34**: 605–632 (1988).

175. NATIONAL INSTITUTE ON DRUG ABUSE. Mandatory guidelines for federal workplace drug testing programs: final guidelines. *Federal register,* **53**: 11 970–11 989 (1988).

176. *Health promotion in the workplace: alcohol and drug abuse. Report of a WHO Expert Committee.* Geneva, World Health Organization, 1993 (WHO Technical Report Series, No. 833).

177. KAPUR B. Drug testing methods and interpretations of test results. *In:* Macdonald, S. & Roman, P., ed. *Research advances in alcohol and drug problems. Vol. II. Drug testing in the workplace.* New York and London, Plenum Press, 1994, pp. 103–120.

178. WINEK, C.L. & PAUL, L.J. Effects of short-term storage conditions on alcohol concentration in blood from living human subjects. *Clinical chemistry,* **29**: 1959–1960 (1983).

179. ROTHMAN, M. Random drug testing in the workplace: implications for human resource management. *Business horizons,* March/April 1988, pp. 23–27.

180. HARGER, R.N. ET AL. The partition ratio of alcohol between air and water, urine and blood. Estimation and identification of alcohol in those liquids from analysis of air equilibrated with them. *Journal of biological chemistry,* **183**: 197–213 (1950).

181. O'NEILL, B. Variability in blood alcohol concentrations. *Journal of studies on alcohol,* **44**: 222–230 (1983).

182. DUBOWSKI, K.M. Studies in breath-alcohol analysis: biological factors. *Zeitschrift für Rechtmedizin,* **76**: 93–117 (1975).

183. SIMPSON, G. Accuracy and precision of breath-alcohol measurements for a random subject in the postabsorptive state. *Clinical chemistry,* **32**: 261–268 (1987).

184. PAYNE, J.P. ET AL. Observations on distribution of alcohol in blood, breath and urine. *British medical journal,* **1**: 196–202 (1966).

185. ROTHSTEIN, M.A. *Medical screening and the employee health cost crisis.* Washington, DC, Bureau of National Affairs, 1989.

186. BARNUM, D.T. & GLEASON, J.M. The credibility of drug tests: a multi-stage bayesian analysis. *Industrial and labor relations review,* **74**(4): 610–621 (1994).

187. OSTERLOH, J. & BECKER, C.E. Chemical dependency and drug testing in the workplace. *West journal of medicine,* **152**: 506–513 (1990).

188. CASTRO, J. ET AL. Battling with the enemy within. *Time,* 17 March 1986, pp. 52–61.

189. WILLETTE, R.E. Drug testing programs. *In: Urine testing for drugs abuse.* Washington, DC, US Government Printing Office, 1986 (NIDA Research Monograph No. 73).

190. EICHLER, S. ET AL. *Operation "Red Block": case study of a peer prevention substance abuse program for railroad industry personnel.* Rockville, MD, Institute for Human Resources, 1988.

191. JONES, J.P. Drug testing did not reduce Southern Pacific's accident rate. *Forensic urine drug testing,* June 1990, pp. 2–4.

192. SHERIDAN, J. & WINKLER, H. An evaluation of drug testing in the workplace. *In: Drugs in the workplace: research and evaluation data.* Washington, DC, US Government Printing Office, 1989 (NIDA Research Monograph No. 91).

193. DECRESCE, R.P. ET AL. *Drug testing in the workplace.* Chicago, IL, American Society of Clinical Pathologists, 1989.

194. SEGAL, J.A. How reasonable is your suspicion? *Personnel administrator,* December 1989, pp. 103–104.

195. DUPONT, R.L. Mandatory random testing needs to be undertaken at the worksite. *In:* Engs, R.C., ed. *Controversies in the addictions field. Vol. 1.* Dubuque, IA, Kendall/Hunt Publishing Company, 1990, pp. 105–111.

196. FAY, J. *Drug testing.* Stonham, MA, Butterworth-Heinemann, 1991.

197. *International information exchange on drugs in the workplace.* Geneva, International Labour Office, 1991.

198. O'KEEFE, A.M. The case against drug testing. *Psychology today,* June 1987, pp. 34–38.

199. ROTHSTEIN, M.A. Medical screening and employment law: A note of caution and some observations. *Employment testing,* 3: 363–369 (1989).

200. WEEKS, J.L. Eight problems examined that point out serious inadequacies in testing for drug abuse. *Mining engineering,* 39: 999–1002 (1987).

201. CRANT, J.M. & BATEMAN, T.S. An experimental test of the impact of drug-testing programs on potential job applicants' attitudes and intentions. *Journal of applied psychology,* 75: 127–131 (1989).

202. AXEL, H. Characteristics of forms with drugs testing programs. *In: Drugs in the workplace: research and evaluation data.* Washington, DC, US Government Printing Office, 1989 (NIDA Research Monograph No. 91).

203. MASI, D.A. & BURNS, L.E. Urinalysis testing and EAPs. *EAP digest,* 6: 37–43 (1986).

204. *1993 AMA survey on workplace drug testing and drug abuse policies.* New York, American Management Association, 1993.

205. ZEESE, K.B. *Drug testing legal manual: release #9, August.* New York, Clark Boardman, 1993.

206. CORNISH, C.M. Overview of drug use and drug testing. *In: Drugs and alcohol in the workplace: testing and privacy.* Wilmette, IL, Callaghan and Company, 1988, pp. 33–50.

207. SMITH, J.P. *Alcohol and drugs in the workplace: attitudes, policies and programmes in the European Community.* Geneva, International Labour Office, 1993.

208. INDUSTRIAL RELATIONS SERVICE. Alcohol awareness at work 1: introducing an alcohol policy. *IRS employment trends,* No. 517, pp. 5–12 (1992).

209. KILICH, S. & PLANT, M.A. Regional variations in the level of alcohol-related problems in Britain. *British journal of alcohol,* 76: 47–62 (1981).

210. *Health update 3: alcohol.* London, Health Education Authority, 1993.

211. INDUSTRIAL RELATIONS SERVICE. Alcohol awareness at work 2: alcohol policy provisions. *IRS employment trends,* No. 518, pp. 5–10 (1992).

212. INDUSTRIAL RELATIONS SERVICE. Alcohol awareness at work 3: implementation and effectiveness. *IRS employment trends,* No. 519, pp. 7–12 (1992).

213. HOWIE, G. & CARTER, H. Survey of the implementation of workplace alcohol and smoking policies among employers in Fife. *Health bulletin,* **50**(2): 151–155 (1992).

214. HORE, B.D. & PLANT, M.A. *Alcohol problems in employment.* London, Croom-Helm, 1980.

215. DOMMASCHK-RUMP, C. & WOHLFARTH, U. Alcohol at working place – superiors express their views. *Sucht,* **37**: 167–174 (1991).

216. *Don't mix it: drinking and work – the facts.* London, Health Education Authority, 1993.

217. *Don't mix it: user guide.* London, Health Education Authority, 1993.

218. BICKERTON, R. *Clearing house for EAP information.* Arlington, VA, Association of Labor-Management Administrators and Consultants on Alcoholism, 1988.

219. JOEMAN, L.M. Alcohol at work: the cost to employers. *Employment gazette,* December 1991, pp. 669–680.

220. GODFREY, C. ET AL. Alcohol costs and workplace policies: two surveys of employers. *Addiction research,* **1**(3): 239–255 (1993).

221. GODFREY, C. Alcohol in the workplace – a costly problem? *Alcoholism,* **3**: 1–3 (1992).

222. CHADWICK, K. & PENDLETON, L. *The effects of alcohol in the workplace: a survey of small and medium businesses in Liverpool.* Liverpool, Merseyside Regional Alcohol Coordinator Scheme, 1993.

223. ALCOHOL CONCERN. Alcohol and the workplace: policies, perspectives and problems. *Acquire,* No. 8, pp. 10–11 (1994).

224. DEUTSCHE HAUPTSTELLE GEGEN DIE SUCHTGEFAHREN. *Jahrbuch Sucht.* Geesthacht, Neuland-Verlagsgesellschaft mbH, 1992.

225. DEUTSCHE HAUPTSTELLE GEGEN DIE SUCHTGEFAHREN. *Jahrbuch Sucht.* Geesthacht, Neuland-Verlagsgesellschaft mbH, 1993.

226. SPRINGER, A. Alkoholismus am Arbeitsplatz – ökonomische und gesundheitspolitische Bedeutung der betrieblichen Früherkennung. *Wiener Zeitschrift für Suchtforschung,* **16**(1): 5–9 (1993).

227. FUCHS, R. & RUMMEL, M. Chemical dependency at work and organisational development: a management training programme aimed at the superiors of an institute for financial services. *In:* Bellabarba, J. et al., ed. *Chemical dependency at work employees assistance programmes (substance abuse). Our work in the context of Company Internal Health Promotion Programmes.* Berlin, Landesstelle Berlin gegen die Suchtgefahren, 1993, pp. 2–10.

228. DINARDO, J. A critical review of the estimates of the costs of alcohol and drug use. *In:* Macdonald, S. & Roman, P.M., ed. *Research advances in alcohol and drug problems. Vol. II. Drug testing in the workplace.* New York, Plenum Press, 1994, pp. 57–76.

229. KOLB, L. *Drug addiction: a medical problem.* Springfield, IL, Charles C. Thomas, 1962.

230. O'DONNELL, J.A. *Narcotics addicts in Kentucky.* Chevy Chase, MD, National Institute of Mental Health (US Public Health Service Publication No. 1881).

231. PLAYOUST, D. ET AL. Diminution ou arrêt de la consommation alcoolique. *Bulletin du HCEIA,* **1**: 39–50 (1988).

232. CHOQUET, M. & LEDOUX, S. French report. *In:* Plant, M., ed. *Alcohol-related problems in high-risk groups.* Copenhagen, WHO Regional Office for Europe, 1989 (EURO Reports and Studies, No. 109).

233. GUYOT, F. Les études existantes (parties 1 et 2). *In: Approche des coûts sanitaires et sociaux de l'alcoolisme.* Paris, Haut comité d'études et d'information sur l'alcoolisme, 1985.